The Message of Ruth

The Wings of Refuge

'May those who sow in tears reap with shouts of joy!'
(Psalm 126:5)

David Atkinson
Chaplain, Corpus Christi College, Oxford

Inter-Varsity Press
Leicester, England
Downers Grove, Illinois, U.S.A.

Inter-Varsity Press
38 De Montfort Street, Leicester LE1 7GP, England
P.O. Box 1400, Downers Grove, Illinois 60515, USA

© David Atkinson 1983

Unless otherwise stated, quotations from the Bible are from the Revised Standard Version, copyrighted 1946, 1952, © 1971, 1973, by the Division of Christian Education, National Council of the Churches of Christ in the USA, and used by permission.

The poem on p. 55, 'Love's as warm as tears' from *Poems* by C. S. Lewis, is reproduced by permission of William Collins Sons & Co. Ltd.

First published 1983
(under the title 'The Wings of Refuge')

Reprinted 1984, 1985, 1988, 1989, 1991, 1993
(under the title 'The Message of Ruth: The Wings of Refuge')

UK ISBN 0–85110–740–0
USA ISBN 0–87784–294–9

Set in 10/11 Garamond by
Nuprint Services Ltd, Harpenden, Herts
Printed in England by Clays Ltd, St Ives plc

Inter-Varsity Press is the book-publishing division of the Universities and Colleges Christian Fellowship (formerly the Inter-Varsity Fellowship), a student movement linking Christian Unions in universities and colleges throughout the United Kingdom and the Republic of Ireland, and a member movement of the International Fellowship of Evangelical Students. For information about local and national activities write UCCF, 38 De Montfort Street, Leicester LE1 7GP.

InterVarsity Press, USA, is the book-publishing division of InterVarsity Christian Fellowship, a student movement active on campus at hundreds of universities, colleges and schools of nursing in the United States of America, and a member movement of the International Fellowship of Evangelical Students. For information about local and regional activities, write Public Relations Dept., InterVarsity Christian Fellowship, 6400 Schroeder Rd., P.O. Box 7895, Madison, WI 53707-7895.

Distributed in Canada through InterVarsity Press, 860 Dension St., Unit 3, Markham, Ontario L3R 4H1, Canada.

The Bible speaks today

Series Editors: J. A. Motyer (OT)
John R. W. Stott (NT)

The Message of Ruth
The Wings of Refuge

Titles in this series

General preface

The Bible speaks today describes a series of both Old Testament and New Testament expositions, which are characterized by a threefold ideal: to expound the biblical text with accuracy, to relate it to contemporary life, and to be readable.

These books are, therefore, not 'commentaries', for the commentary seeks rather to elucidate the text than to apply it, and tends to be a work rather of reference than of literature. Nor, on the other hand, do they contain the kind of 'sermons' which attempt to be contemporary and readable, without taking Scripture seriously enough.

The contributors to this series are all united in their convictions that God still speaks through what he has spoken, and that nothing is more necessary for the life, health and growth of Christians than that they should hear what the Spirit is saying to them through his ancient – yet ever modern – Word.

J. A. MOTYER
J. R. W. STOTT
Series Editors

For Suzan

Contents

Author's preface

It is a number of years since I first tried out some sermons from the book of Ruth on the congregation of Smithills Hall Chapel, Bolton, where it was my privilege to serve as Curate. I found myself preaching about Naomi, and the way God held on to her, at a time of personal upheaval in my own life and in our family. I discovered that Naomi's God also held on to us, and that I was learning to give much richer meaning to words like 'providence' and 'grace' than I ever had before.

We moved from Bolton to St John's, Harborne, Birmingham, and good friends there also encouraged me to expound parts of the book of Ruth at the midweek church gathering. Many kindnesses shown to us then reinforced my conviction that God's care for us is most often perceived and received through the care of others. Boaz well illustrates how the pattern of God's faithful love to his people is meant to be the pattern of our relationships with one another. From this side of the incarnation, and of Calvary and the empty tomb, we are able to fill out in much richer detail than ever the author of Ruth could have understood, something of the meaning of redemptive grace and faithful love.

Working more recently on the book of Ruth, what has often come to the fore in my mind is the deep faith of its author, and the way in which he, or she, confidently believes that all things fall within the providential care of a gracious God. It is this conviction that I have been helped to learn a little more clearly in the harder times: that in Christ, God gives us what we need to help us cope with uncertainties. That, I think, is part of the meaning of faith.

May God use these expositions to help others discover more of his gracious care, and to feel more at home under the 'refuge of his wings'.

DAVID ATKINSON

Chief abbreviations

AV	The Authorized (King James) Version of the Bible, 1611.
Cooke	G. A. Cooke, *Ruth* (*The Cambridge Bible*, CUP, 1918).
Eichrodt	W. Eichrodt, *Theology of the Old Testament*, 1 (ET, SCM Press, 1961).
JB	The Jerusalem Bible (Darton, Longman and Todd, 1966).
Keil-Delitzsch	C. F. Keil and F. Delitzsch, *Biblical Commentary on the Old Testament: Ruth* (ET, Eerdmans, 1968).
Knight	G. A. Knight, *Ruth and Jonah* (*Torch Bible Commentaries*, SCM Press, 1950).
Knox	*The New Testament of our Lord and Saviour Jesus Christ* translated by Ronald Knox (Burns, Oates and Washbourne, 1946).
Leggett	D. A. Leggett, *The Levirate and Goel Institutions in the Old Testament* (Mack, NJ, 1974).
Moffatt	*The New Testament: a New Translation* by James Moffatt (Hodder and Stoughton, revised edition, 1935).
Morris	A. E. Cundall and L. Morris, *Judges and Ruth* (*Tyndale Old Testament Commentaries*, Inter-Varsity Press, 1968).
NEB	The New English Bible (NT 1961, [2]1970; OT 1970).
NIV	The New International Version of the Bible (Hodder and Stoughton, 1979).
Rowley	H. H. Rowley, 'The Marriage of Ruth' in *The Servant of the Lord and Other Essays* (Blackwell, [2]1965).

RSV	The Revised Standard Version of the Bible (NT 1946, ^{2}1971; OT 1952).
RV	The Revised Version of the Bible (1884).
De Vaux	Roland de Vaux, *Ancient Israel* (Darton, Longman and Todd, ^{3}1973).

Introduction

Providence?

'It's evening, and it's dark, and I'm afraid.' So says the judge to the priest in Bergman's film *The Rite,* crying into the unknown the fear, the silence and the loneliness of a great deal of our broken twentieth-century world. In another of his films, *The Seventh Seal,* one of the characters, searching, maybe, for a clue to the meaning of some of the questions and uncertainties of life, and of death, says, 'We make an idol of our fear, and call it God.'

Bergman's voice, from the uncertainty and dread of life lived only from within the perspective of this natural order, or at least from a perspective within which the question 'Where are you, God?' never seems to bring a reply, is speaking for many others in whom a living faith in God, and in his gracious interaction with his world, has been extinguished. Their eyes see only the flow and counter-flow of events and experiences; their minds can discern no pattern or meaning; and they have lost hold of, or have never reached out to grasp, the hand of the unseen God who rules all, plans all, and whose purposes give meaning to history both on world and on individual levels.

By contrast, faith in the providence of God (the general name that Christians have given to God's present activity in the world) is very much alive in the main characters, and in the unknown author, of the little book of Ruth. The story is set 'in the days when the judges ruled',[1] days when, as we shall see, faith in God was threatened by much that was 'dark' and 'fear-making'. But even in a context in which faith was challenged, our author urges upon his readers – upon us – a certainty, and delight, in the security of God's providence.

[1] Ruth 1:1 (literally: 'when the judges judged').

11

Before examining the details of the book of Ruth, however, we shall first remind ourselves more fully of what Christians have understood by the term 'providence', and indicate some of the difficulties that stand against such a faith in our day. Then we shall move back to the very different world of twelfth- or eleventh-century BC Palestine, to 'the days when the judges ruled', and shall discover nevertheless that in some ways the challenges to faith in the providence of God were not so very different in those times from what they are now.

The meaning of 'providence' was expressed by Christians of an earlier age like this:

> God the great Creator of all things doth uphold, direct, dispose and govern all creatures, actions and things, from the greatest even to the least, by his most wise and holy providence, according to his infallible foreknowledge, and the free and immutable counsel of his own will, to the praise of the glory of his wisdom, power, justice, goodness and mercy.[2]

Or, to update the language somewhat, Christians have believed that God not only *created* the world so that we his creatures are dependent on him for our existence; he also *sustains* and *rules* his world, so that we are continuously dependent on him for 'life and breath and everything'.[3]

It may be helpful to make certain distinctions at this point between the *creative* and *sustaining* activity of God on the one hand, and his *general* and *special providence* – with which we shall be mostly concerned in Ruth – on the other. Some writers use 'providence' to stand for the activity of God as he guides and governs his created order.[4] In this sense, as Michael Langford notes, providence is already involved in the Christian understanding of creation. 'Within the very notion of the created universe we already have the idea of an order that has its own laws, its own causality, and its own relative independence.'[5] Similarly Christians have spoken of the *sustaining* activity of God as the upholding of this sort of order within which changes and development in creation take place. So in the large sense, 'providence' includes God's sustaining activity also. But it is in a slightly more restricted sense that 'providence' is usually used, namely, to describe 'the guiding or steering of nature, man, and history'.[6] It is in this sense we shall use it when we come to Ruth.

---

[2] *Westminster Confession*, chapter 5, section 1.   [3] Acts 17:25.
[4] Michael J. Langford, *Providence* (SCM Press, 1981), p. 4.
[5] *Ibid.*, p. 7.   [6]*Ibid.*, p. 23.

Many Christian writers find it helpful to distinguish between *general providence* and *special providence*. The former 'refers to the government of the universe through universal laws that control or influence the world without the need for specific or *ad hoc* acts of divine will'.[7] The latter, special providence, concerns specific events which are understood by the man of faith to be particular evidence of God's activity. 'Providence' thus indicates *a particular sort of interpretation* put upon events and upon nature, man and history. For clarity, we need to distinguish 'providence' from 'miracle' – best kept to refer to a non-repeatable counter-instance of an otherwise demonstrable law of nature. By contrast, 'providence' is 'the guidance or steering of nature, man and history; it is not the manipulation of these orders by the introduction of causal factors which would lead a scientist to be mystified.'[8]

A faith in providence thus recognizes the creaturely dependence of the world, and also its *contingency*, that is, God could have created it different. 'Providence' acknowledges both God's sovereign lordship in his world, and man's freedom to live responsibly within God's limits. 'For Christians, the world and history are not ultimately meaningful in themselves, but in relation to God and his purposes.'[9] All God's interaction with his world – whether by choosing Abraham to father a nation; by establishing his covenant on Sinai; by the events of the birth and life and death and resurrection of Jesus Christ; by the establishment of the Christian church and the outpouring of the Holy Spirit; in the contemporary experience of Christians – all God's interactions with the world at the global and the personal levels are in line with his over-all purpose for his creation 'to share his life and love and glory with another reality over which he would be Lord.'[10] This God, so Christians believe, revealed in Christ and attested in the Scriptures, is there; he cares, he rules, he provides.

In such a view of God there are extremes to be avoided. For example, *deism* separates God from his world entirely: he has wound it up, so it is thought, and is now letting it run. *Pantheism* confuses God with everything that he has made. Christian faith, by contrast with both extremes, understands God to be distinct from and greater than his creation, but intimately involved with it at every point. Equally, against the Epicurean notion that the world is ultimately an accident

---

[7] *Ibid.*, p.11.   [8] *Ibid.*, p. 23.

[9] P. Forster, 'Providence and Prayer', in T. F. Torrance (ed.), *Belief in Science and in Christian Life* (Handsel Press, 1980), p. 111.

[10] *Ibid.*

of chance (a view still widely believed),[11] and also against the Stoic teaching that we are in the hands of a blind fate, Christians have believed that the living, personal, rational, holy, loving Creator God sustains and rules his world.

Such belief in God's providence gives a firm standpoint from which to seek to understand the world. We do not see the glories and tragedies of national and global events, and the joys and the pains of day-to-day family life, as finding their meaning only within human history, or personal biography. Their true meaning lies within the purposes of a God who has made himself known as loving and holy, as personal and infinite, as Creator and Redeemer, as Sustainer and Ruler.

Human joys are thus enriched. At the level of personal devotion, one hymn-writer put it this way:

> Heaven above is softer blue,
> Earth around is sweeter green;
> Something lives in every hue,
> Christless eyes have never seen:
> Birds with gladder songs o'erflow,
> Flowers with deeper beauties shine,
> Since I know, as now I know,
> I am his, and he is mine.[12]

But the uncertainties of life, too, are brought within the context of a faith by which they may be coped with:

> Judge not the Lord by feeble sense,
>   But trust him for his grace;
> Behind a frowning providence
>   He hides a smiling face.[13]

'Providence' says that God is there, God cares, God rules, and God provides. Faith in such a God undergirds every chapter of Ruth.

Challenges to faith

Such a faith as we have described is under threat from many of the

---

[11] A view canvassed eloquently by J. Monod in *Chance and Necessity* (1970, ET, Collins, 1971).

[12] George Wade Robinson, 'Loved with everlasting love.'

[13] William Cowper, 'God moves in a mysterious way.'

isolating, confusing and fear-making pressures of twentieth-century life. Or perhaps we should say that the doctrine of providence has been neglected. Contrast our present attitudes with what J. H. Newman said a hundred years ago: 'What Scripture especially illustrates from its first page to its last, is God's Providence, and that is nearly the only doctrine held with a real assent by the mass of religious Englishmen.'[14]

Not only has our century experienced world wars of immense destruction, and is under growing pressure to expect and prepare for another, it is also beset by other enormous apocalyptic questions which threaten to change the whole notion of what it means to be human. The slaughter of unborn infants on an unprecedented scale makes Canaanite child-sacrifice seem almost insignificant by comparison. Not only so, while recognizing the many social pressures which lie behind many requests for termination of pregnancy, abortion is often discussed only in terms of 'rights' and 'benefits' for the already born. This is having a profound effect on our social consciousness concerning what traditionally has been thought of as life's 'sanctity'. Many arguments for abortion lead logically to justification of infanticide. There is increasing pressure to enforce so-called 'death with dignity' on the aged, and to withhold life from some infants born handicapped. Hundreds of millions of people in our world are being starved by neglect through the sustained affluence of the West, and because the so-called 'powers' prefer to use the under-privileged as political pawns rather than set themselves to solve the problems of a just distribution of the rich bounty of God's earth.

All this and more calls in question what Christians have traditionally proclaimed: that each person is precious because he or she is made as 'the image of God'. The availability of technology for contraception (which like all other benefits is capable of misuse), coupled with media and other pressures towards so-called 'permissiveness', increasingly makes for a total separation between the unitive and the procreative aspects of sexual intercourse, and between sexual intercourse and heterosexual marriage, thus challenging the traditional Christian understanding of the meaning of man-womanhood.[15] The increasing promise of what we *can* do in scientific and biomedical research, without corresponding thought concerning what we *may* do;[16] the power of multinational monopolies to engulf the concerns and rights of individual people – these in their own ways pose the question,

[14] J. H. Newman, *The Grammar of Assent,* quoted in T. F. Torrance (ed.), *Belief in Science and in Christian Life,* p. 110.

[15] *Cf.* Paul Ramsey, *One Flesh* (Grove, 1975).

[16] *Cf.* references in D. J. Atkinson, *The Values of Science* (Grove, 1980).

'What is a human being?' And the scourge of racism threatens violence and war in many places.

G. C. Berkouwer has written:

> Shall not the twentieth century, though productive of much that is good, always remain the century of the concentration camps and the pogroms, of war and hatred, of attack on the worth of humanity itself? And must we not bate our breath for what is to come?[17]

And then he rightly asks,

> Does the Gospel have meaning and worth for our time? Does the Church have the courage and the right to preach the living God in the midst of *this* senseless world?[18]

Atheism seems to many to be the only logical and permissible conclusion to draw from the evidence of our times.

From this discussion, we can isolate three factors in particular which have posed a challenge to faith in the providence of God: other gods, a split culture, and the problem of evil.

Other gods

It is not only that 'modern man does not believe in the reality of God', but more positively put, 'a pervasive cultural atheism' is in fact the underlying faith of the age.[19] This faith, secularism, reflects an understanding of man as totally master of his own destiny, of material things as the ultimate source of values, and of the natural order as comprising the whole of reality. Man-centredness in human relationships, materialism in human values, and the belief that this world is all there is – these are the characteristics of modern man's faith. So live and make merry, for tomorrow we die. It is true that alongside this faith there is often expressed the longing for significance in the 'evening', the darkness and the fear: 'We die only once, and for such a long time.' But 'pervasive cultural atheism' nonetheless dominates our world, and these other gods – humanism, materialism, naturalism – pose a strong challenge to a Christian's understanding of the providence of God.

[17] G. C. Berkouwer, *The Providence of God* (Eerdmans, 1961; Inter-Varsity Press, 1973), p. 8.

[18] *Ibid.*, pp. 8f.

[19] H. W. Richardson, *Theology for a New World* (SCM Press, 1967), p. 1.

A split culture

The growth of modern science, its development into scientism (the idea that science has the key to all knowledge), and the achievements of modern technology, have been the bridges to unbelief in God for many. As 'Nature' (a word which used to carry overtones of God's purposes for the natural world) became identified with 'natural causes', so we no longer pray for our daily bread, but instead (rather than 'as well') put effort into crop cultivation and bakery efficiency. Whereas Addison believed

> The spacious firmament on high,
> With all the blue ethereal sky,
> And spangled heavens, a shining frame,
> Their great Original proclaim,[20]

as did the psalmist ('The heavens are telling the glory of God; and the firmament proclaims his handiwork'),[21] we know better. The black holes, red giants, white dwarfs, and multi-million-dollar space programmes make the 'Great Original' sound rather archaic as well as improbable. And there are many whose increasing understanding of the universe is coupled not with a deeper worship, but with a deeper scepticism. Steven Weinberg, author of *The First Three Minutes*, concludes: 'The more the universe seems comprehensible, the more it also seems pointless.'[22]

Although, of course, many of the scientific community are alert to the limitations of the scientific method, indeed to the very human place of the human knowing subject in the processes of science,[23] and to the ethical questions increasingly being raised by new technological possibilities,[24] our culture has become overwhelmed by the apparent irrelevance of God to our thought-life and actual morality.[25] This is

[20] J. Addison, 'The spacious firmament on high.'

[21] Ps. 19:1.

[22] Steven Weinberg, *The First Three Minutes* (Fontana Collins, 1977), p. 149.

[23] *Cf. e.g.* M. Polanyi, *Personal Knowledge* (Routledge and Kegan Paul, 1958), and other writings.

[24] *Cf. e.g.* D. Morley, *The Sensitive Scientist* (SCM Press, 1978).

[25] Although, as A. R. Peacocke puts it (*Science and the Christian Experiment*, OUP, 1971, pp. 133f.): 'The realization that our minds can find the world intelligible, and the implication this has that an explanation for the world process is to be found in mental rather than purely material categories, has been for many scientists who are theists . . . an essential turning point in their thinking. Why *should* science work at all? That it does so points strongly to a principle of rationality, to an interpretation of the

true of the way we think of global and national concerns. It is also true of the way we organize our family priorities. Even among Christians, the 'Christian mind'[26] has all but disappeared, and many ethical decisions are taken on the basis of a Christianized hedonism ('what makes us feel so good must be God's will'), or a Christianized utilitarianism (which measures 'what God wills' only by the amount of 'benefit' an action brings). In his book *God Alive*, Bishop Leonard rightly notes that 'it is not an exaggeration to say that the average Christian today sees religion primarily in terms of the help which God can give him or her in this world, with a vague expectation for the world to come, rather than as an active creative relationship with God; a relationship which has professional implications for this life but which is fulfilled in eternity. To put it crudely, it is an attitude which regards God in terms of his usefulness rather than as the object of adoration and love.'[27]

A 'utilitarian positivism' (concentrating primarily on observable facts which are likely to be useful) is increasingly also becoming a dominant view of the nature of science. The question remains to be answered whether science cut free from its roots in the Christian tradition within which it came first to birth[28] can last without dissolving into no more than a secularized technology in which cost-benefit becomes more important than truth.[29] Furthermore, in some scientific work, on test-tube babies, for example, we seem also to be hearing the researcher's variant of the song 'It feels so right that it can't be wrong'.

In such a milieu, it is not surprising that a schizophrenic split has taken place: the 'religious' aspects of life are separated off from the world of our everyday concerns. This is sometimes seen in the mystical flight into subjective religious experiences which can so lose contact with the objective ground of faith that they become emotionally

cosmos in terms of mind as its most signficant feature. Any thinking which takes science seriously must, it seems to me, start from this . . . There is clearly a kinship between the mind of man and the cosmos which is real, and which any account of the cosmos cannot ignore.'

I myself would prefer to say 'personal' and 'personhood' rather than 'mental', 'mind': but the point remains.

[26] H. Blamires, *The Christian Mind* (SPCK, 1963).

[27] G. Leonard, *God Alive* (Darton, Longman and Todd, 1981), pp. 17f.

[28] *Cf.* P. E. Hodgson, 'The Judaeo-Christian Origin of Science', *Ampleforth Journal* LXXIX (1974).

[29] W. A. Thorson, 'The Spiritual Dimensions of Science', in C. F. H. Henry (ed.), *Horizons of Science* (Harper and Row, 1978), pp. 217f., and others quoted in D. J. Atkinson, *The Values of Science*.

equivalent to other consciousness-enhancing experiences, except that they use 'God-talk' to describe them. Sometimes the split is seen in the pietistic withdrawal from 'the world', thought of as an evil place, into a 'purer' environment of 'spiritual' concerns and individual personal faith only. In the flight into subjectivism we see how the emphasis on experience for experience's sake has become detached from an under-standing of God's truth as an objective revelation. In pietism there is often at one and the same time both a reverence for God's word of revelation and yet also the imposition upon it of a sundering, alien to the mind of the Bible, between the world of the spirit and the world of every day – frequently with lines of 'separation' drawn by arbitrary convention or tradition.

This cultural split, separating off 'religion' from the subject matter of history and science, poses a threat to the unified understanding of life and the world which used to be, and still can be, possible by belief in the providence of God.

The problem of evil

Undoubtedly the greatest threat to belief in the providence of God is the reality of evil in our world. Not only the concentration camps and the pogroms, but the pain of bereavement, the headlines of another devastating famine or hurricane, the gross inequalities of opportunity and fortune in different parts of the world, our neighbour's cancer – all these pose the question: 'Where is God?' How, in a world where so much evil is apparently meaningless, can we maintain faith in God's providential sustenance and rule? For the Christian believer, part of the meaning of faith is that it is God's gift to enable us to cope with the uncertainties, and apparent meaninglessness – what the Preacher called the 'vanity'[30] – of much of this broken world's history. But to pretend that such faith never feels itself to be threatened by the sometimes unspeakable evil of man to man, or by the hazards of 'nature', is to be either blissfully overprotected or wilfully obtuse.

There are many things this side of heaven the meaning of which is hidden in the mystery of God. There are many experiences many of us would very much rather not have gone through. Though much that is evil can be understood in terms of the sinful abandonment by men of the patterns of life which, so Christian faith has taught, embody the will of God, there is much for which there is no human explanation or cause. Our faith in the providence of God must be large enough to

[30] Ec. 1:2,14.

cope with these uncertainties, and large enough to handle the painful and sometimes bitter feelings to which they give rise. As we shall see, the characters of the book of Ruth also had uncertainties to face. We shall learn, too, how faith in God was to them a gift which helped them cope.

'In the days of the judges'

The details of twentieth-century life differ in so many ways from those of twelfth- or eleventh-century BC Palestine, that to open the book of Ruth, set in this period of the judges of Israel, is to walk into another world. And yet the believers in Yahweh, the name by which they had been invited to know their God,[31] were at that time themselves facing a period of unprecedented challenge to their faith.

Israel had come through years of upheaval. At the exodus their God had, as they believed, rescued them from slavery in Egypt. After their wilderness years, he had preserved them through the wars of conquest and ushered them into possession of their promised land. But the confederacy of Israel's tribes was hardly settled in faith. The people of God, now in Canaan, were struggling to adjust to a farming style of life, and to becoming one among the nations. B. W. Anderson calls this the 'struggle between faith and culture'.[32] Using headings similar to those we have used for our day, we can isolate the main pressures exerted on the Israelite believer by the temptations of his surrounding Canaanite culture.

[31] Yahweh was the personal name of the covenant God, the significance of which was made known to Moses; Ex. 6:2 (cf. J. A. Motyer, *The Revelation of the Divine Name*, Tyndale Monograph, 1959). It expressed 'the idea of existence'; 'This is certainly not a matter of Being in the metaphysical sense of aseity, absolute existence, pure self-determination or any other ideas of the same kind. It is concerned with a revelation of the divine will, which God grants to Moses when he entrusts him with the good news "I am that I am" — that is to say "I am really and truly present, ready to help and act, as I have always been."'... What is stressed is not a general existence at all times and places, but existence here and now.' *The emphasis is not on passive, but on active existence* (W. Eichrodt, *Theology of the Old Testament*, 1, ET, SCM Press, 1961, p. 190). 'The new divine name proclaimed by Moses agrees in a remarkable way with the earlier Hebrew designations of God' (*Ibid.*) in its opposition to all that is merely naturalistic, in indicating a controlling and effective reality, in speaking of God's real presence in being associated in later Israelite faith with the concept of eternity. Yahweh is God's personal name, especially linked with his character as the covenant God of Israel. His name is rendered by 'LORD' in RSV.

[32] B. W. Anderson, *The Living World of the Old Testament* (Longmans, [2]1967), chapter 4.

Other gods

Like people today, the Canaanites of old were absorbed in finding the secret of prosperity. What would make the economy sound? What would guarantee full employment? What would provide an adequate living wage, and maintain living standards? Since their economy was predominantly agricultural, their pursuit of prosperity focused on the need for fertile land abounding in crops, fertile flocks and herds, and a fertile marriage providing in due course workers and inheritors for the farm. Religion was, in their view, the key to prosperity. Only God could create fertility, in particular the god Baal, which means 'lord' or 'owner'. Baal was the name of the male deity. In Canaanite belief he owned the land and controlled its fertility. His female partner was Ashtart (pl. Ashtaroth).[33] The Baal and the Ashtart were understood both as cosmic deities who dwelt in the heavens, and also as associated with particular localities. The regular cycle of nature and the fertility of the ground, the new life of spring following the barrenness of winter, were due to sexual intercourse between Baal and his female partner.

Man was not a mere spectator in this marriage of the gods. It was obviously desperately important that the gods should not lapse into forgetfulness on this vital matter, and the technique employed to bring earth's needs constantly to their minds was that of 'imitative magic'. People would perform on earth the acts equivalent to those they wished the gods to perform in heaven. For this reason, the shrines of Baal, often located on bare hill-top heights in order to have the best chance of catching the eye of the gods, were scenes of orgiastic sexual rites. Girls and men alike enrolled in the service of the god and copulated freely with male and female worshippers.

Such a religion proved appealing to Israel newly involved in an agricultural way of life. As Anderson notes,[34] it is not surprising that the Israelites, unaccustomed to the ways of agriculture, were tempted to turn to the gods of the land.

In fact, of course, in Israelite understanding, fertility on the land and prosperity among the people were part of the promised blessings associated with the covenant by which Yahweh had called them to be his family. The enjoyment of those blessings of fertility and prosperity was linked to the covenant obligations on the people of Yahweh, to live in responsive obedience to Yahweh's known will. This principle, enshrined most clearly perhaps in the blessing and cursings of Deuteronomy chapter 28, is the pattern of the covenant from the earliest

[33] *Cf.* Jdg. 2:13; 10:6.   [34] Anderson, *Living World*, pp. 102f.

days: 'I will be your God; you will be my people.'[35] 'All these blessings shall come upon you and overtake you, if you obey the voice of the Lord your God.'[36] But the lure of other gods was strong.

The lure today is not that of imitative magic to jog Baal's memory. It is rather the lure of the vain belief that 'economic laws', 'monetarist policies', 'free collective bargaining', 'nationalization', or whatever, will of themselves create prosperity if we will only bow down to them and worship them. We too easily forget that obedient holiness in response to the known will of God is always a key factor in social strength, harmony and prosperity. As British Trades Union Congress General Secretary Len Murray commented on the reissue of William Temple's book *Christianity and Social Order:* 'It is a permanent reminder of the truth of R. A. Butler's words that "Untouched by morality and idealism economics is an arid pursuit, and politics an unprofitable one."'[37] If for 'morality' we substitute 'holiness', and for 'idealism' we substitute 'spiritual concerns', the point is stronger still. The fundamental problems at the heart of national life are not economic or political, but spiritual: a failure to see that the worship of economic or political theory is an idolatry which blinds us to the living God. As in the days when the judges ruled, so today, faith in the providence of God cannot walk comfortably hand in hand with the lure of other gods.

A *split culture*

Religion has often been used to maintain the *status quo.*[38] For those who are comfortable, religion can easily be invoked as divine sanction for staying comfortable. And the Baal worshipper was no exception. Religion for him, with its central concerns with fertility, was about preserving and enhancing the perpetual cycle of nature. The aim of the gods was to preserve the established order, and religion thus had an interest in maintaining it. The Baal worshipper, through his imitative magic, sought to control the gods to that end. Not so the Israelite understanding of Yahweh!

Yahweh had made himself known in history, in the one non-recurring exodus event and in the establishment of his covenant. Yahweh is the living God who reveals himself in action as the Lord of

---

[35] *Cf.* Gn. 17:7; Ex. 19:4ff.; *etc.*   [36] Dt. 28:1ff.

[37] Cover comment on W. Temple, *Christianity and Social Order,* first published 1942, new edition with an introduction by Professor R. H. Preston, and a Foreword from Edward Heath (SPCK, 1976).

[38] *Cf.* G. E. Wright, *The Old Testament against its Environment* (SCM Press, 1950), p. 44.

history, and whose involvement in the ordinary processes of human living offer a constant challenge to the *status quo* with a call to renewed obedience, and growth in holiness, justice and love. There is no question of the Israelite believer attempting to twist Yahweh's arm! Yahweh's covenant people sought to serve their God in grateful responsive obedience.

In true Israelite spirituality, religious faith and moral life belonged inseparably together. One clear example is the way the very earthy ethical prescriptions of the Holiness Code[39] about domestic, social, economic and agricultural aspects of life, as well as the religious and the cultic, are peppered with reference to God's name: 'I am the LORD.' Because God is who he is ('I AM WHAT I AM'), every aspect of ethical life involves for the Israelite an application of God's nature to the human situtation.

Describing the high points of Israelite spirituality, H. H. Rowley observes:

> The good life... as it is presented to us in the Old Testament, is the life that is lived in harmony with God's will and that expresses itself in daily life in the reflection of the character of God translated into the terms of human experience, that draws its inspiration and its strength from communion with God in the fellowship of his people and in private experience, and that knows how to worship and praise him both in public and in the solitude of the heart.[40]

In the days when the judges ruled, however, people of faith were caught in a tension between the will of Yahweh which they knew had relevance to every area of life, and the existing social order and its cycle of agricultural life-patterns. They were surrounded by the religion of Baal. It seems as though this tension sometimes showed itself in the enticement to make Yahweh more comfortable by keeping him just to a corner of life, and for the rest being open to the more naturalistic approach of the Baal worshipper. This tendency to maintain the service of Yahweh and of Baal side by side was expressed by B. W. Anderson like this: 'To Yahweh they would look in times of military crisis; to Baal they would turn for success in agriculture.'[41]

How easy it can be to make God safe by relegating him just to certain areas of our concerns. But this is the first decisive step towards the cultural split to which we referred earlier, in which the real

[39] Lv. 17 – 26, in particular chapter 19.
[40] H. H. Rowley, *The Faith of Israel* (SCM Press, 1956), p. 149.
[41] Anderson, *Living World*, p. 106.

significance of God and of human life gets lost in the flight into subjectivism and pietism.

There is, of course, a true 'separation' for the people of God, but not in terms of the split between the 'sacred' and the 'secular' with God's interests reserved for the first. Such a way was unfortunately illustrated by the remark of Lord Melbourne, Queen Victoria's first Prime Minister, after hearing an evangelical preacher, that if religion was going to interfere with the affairs of private life, things were come to a pretty pass![42] No, the true separation for God's people is their distinctiveness in their calling to be his covenant family, seen in their corporate and individual responses of loving obedient holiness towards him, and service for their fellow men, expressed in every area of human life and relationship.

Faith in God's providential concern and active involvement in all life does not last long when God is kept 'safe' by keeping him just to a corner, and for the rest seeing what Baal has on offer.

The problem of evil

We should not imagine that the time of the judges was totally faithless! Had time allowed, the writer to the Hebrews would have elaborated more the brief mention we have of the faith of Gideon, Barak, Samson, Jephthah.[43] Far from perfect men, to be sure, but men who knew their God, and in their own different ways showed the reality of a living faith. And they brought some leadership and direction to a people confused and threatened by their new surroundings. But it was short-lived and spasmodic, and there was no lasting stability. It was also a period of great evil. The people's apostasy led to punishment from God.[44] Murder and war, rape and pillage were the order of the day. Enemy scorched-earth policies[45] devastated the agricultural economy.

The second part of the book of Judges[46] paints a grim picture of civil unrest and violence, of social disintegration, of sexual immorality and assault, of war. The people of faith understood this in terms of Yahweh's judgment, and the failure of men to live by Yahweh's ways of righteousness. 'In those days there was no king in Israel; every man did what was right in his own eyes.'[47]

But how can God allow this evil? Where are now the blessings of the covenant? What price now faith in God's providence – his interest and

---

[42] Quoted in Temple, *Christianity and Social Order*, p. 31.
[43] Heb. 11:32.   [44] Jdg. 2:11ff.   [45] Jdg. 6:4ff.
[46] Chapters 17 – 21.   [47] Jdg. 21:25.

concern for every part of life? Such affirmations could have easily worn thin in the minds of those whose lot was simply to be on the receiving end of seemingly endless evil.

The lure of other gods and the temptation to split Yahweh's concerns from everyday life; the social chaos, personal misery, and harsh experience of divine judgment; these are the things which primarily characterize 'the days when the judges ruled'. The scale of the book of Judges is large — national unrest and international strife — and the mood is dark and difficult for the believer in the providence of God.

The book of Ruth

It is into the darkness of these questions that the book of Ruth shines.[48] Although it was written considerably later than the events described,[49] the author sets the story 'in the days when the judges ruled'.[50] It is a tale of charm and delight. According to A. Weiser, Goethe called it 'the loveliest complete work on a small scale, handed down to us as an ethical treatise and an idyll.' He also quotes Rud. Alexander Schröder's verdict: 'No poet in the world has written a more beautiful short story.'[51]

The book of Ruth is a story about very ordinary people facing very ordinary events. We meet Naomi who underwent much hardship in

[48] In the Scriptures as our Lord knew them, Ruth would have appeared as either a preface to the book of Psalms, or an appendix to the book of Judges. Later in the Christian era (probably about the eighth century AD, or a little earlier) Ruth was grouped in the Hebrew Bible together with the other little books among the Hagiographa, as one of the five Rolls which were read at Israelite festivals. Ruth was read at Pentecost. (The others were Song of Songs at Passover, Ecclesiastes at Tabernacles, Esther at Purim, and Lamentations at the anniversary of the destruction of Jerusalem.)

[49] There is considerable difference of opinion concerning the date of the book's composition. Some commentators date it after the exile, in the time of Ezra and Nehemiah. Others bring it much earlier to the time of Solomon. Many believe it is a single narrative; a few, that the form we have now is a late prose edition of a much earlier poem. Ruth 4:7 refers to 'the former times' when a certain now obsolete custom obtains, and there are evidences of the preservation of comparatively early traditions. In reference to the levirate custom, which we discuss later in chapter 5, H. H. Rowley remarks: 'The Book of Ruth then preserves an older usage than the Book of Deuteronomy prescribed. This of course does not mean that the Book of Ruth was written before the Book of Deuteronomy, though neither does it exclude that possibility. It but means that it may preserve a true tradition of pre-Deuteronomic conditions. And this it ought to do if it narrates things that happened centuries before Deuteronomy was written' (Rowley, p. 180).

[50] Ru. 1:1.

[51] A. Weiser, *Introduction to the Old Testament* (Darton, Longman and Todd, 1961), p. 305.

famine and bereavement, but who eventually won through to peace and security. We meet Ruth, the foreign girl from Moab, who attached herself to Naomi her mother-in-law, and to Naomi's God, and received his blessing. We meet Boaz, Naomi's kinsman by marriage, who showed kindness to Ruth and to Naomi, and who by marrying Ruth fits into God's purposes for history – and such a significant history that the great King David[52] and therefore our Lord Jesus Christ himself[53] are numbered among their descendants.

From the many genealogies presented in the Old Testament, we know that right up till the time of Christ, believers in Yahweh had preserved family trees going back over the centuries of their history. It is on such tradition that our author leans. As G. A. F. Knight comments, 'We have no reason to doubt that there was a Naomi who did actually go to Moab with her husband and two sons.'[54] We are, we may judge, dealing with a history. Like every historian, the author of Ruth has selected from the sum total of events, those which best serve his or her purpose in writing.

Precisely what this purpose was has been a matter of dispute among Old Testament specialists. There are many who think that the book was written after the exile, as a reaction to the seemingly harsh views of Ezra and Nehemiah in recalling the people of God back to their exclusiveness; those who had intermarried with foreigners were called back to the faith of their fathers in which such intermarriage was banned.[55] Some of those who had so intermarried now had children. 'Was it the cry of one of those children', asks Knight,[56] 'which brought some completely unknown writer (could it possibly have been a woman?) to write the little pamphlet which we call the Book of Ruth?' Such an explanation is attractive because Ezra seems to have extended the legal prohibition against marriage with Canaanites[57] to prohibition also against Moabites, Ammonites and Egyptians. And Ruth was a Moabitess. If great King David is the offspring of a mixed marriage with a Moabitess, surely Ezra is being too strict in nullifying such marriages? But[58] the legal prohibition in the Torah against intermarriage with Canaanites was a protection against idolatry, and the extension of Ezra's concerns to other idolatrous nations was quite proper, especially in the renewed gathering of the exiled Israel together as a nation again. And after all, the Moabites were forbidden by law to

---

[52] Ru. 4:22.   [53] Mt. 1:5.   [54] Knight, p. 21.
[55] Cf. Ezr. 7:10; 9:1f.; 10:3; Ne. 13:1f., 23.
[56] Knight, p. 21.   [57] Ex. 34:16; Dt. 7:3.
[58] C. F. Keil and F. Delitzsch, *Biblical Commentary on the Old Testament: The Books of Ezra, Nehemiah and Esther* by C. F. Keil (ET, Eerdmans, 1970), p. 116.

enter the congregation.[59] So perhaps the book of Ruth, say some, was a tract against these rulings of the Torah? But all this assumes a late date for the composition of Ruth which is by no means agreed on. And it seems very hard to discern such a polemical intent in the story. Ruth really does not read like a political tract.

Another suggestion is that the book of Ruth was written much earlier than the days of Ezra, during or soon after the days of King David himself. (There was a rabbinic tradition that Samuel was the author, but no-one would argue that now.) Such an earlier date, perhaps in the time of Solomon, might account for the otherwise rather surprising conclusion of the book with a genealogy, which leads up to David himself. There is no textual reason for regarding the genealogy as a later addition. Was a traditional story now committed to writing alongside other literature about the great king?

Alternatively, was the story of Ruth deliberately told to provide an illustration and definition of the concept of 'redemption'? In the course of Ruth we are introduced to various legal practices of the people of ancient Israel relating to family duties and property rights. We shall spend some time looking at the meaning of the *levirate* (concerning marriage customs when the man of the house has died) and especially the *goel* (the 'kinsman-redeemer'). They point to the Israelite understanding of redemption, of land and of people. They illustrate how the law was interpreted, and in what spirit of loving generosity it was applied. And several times the characteristics of the people in this story match what they believed about the character of God. Was it to express his understanding of the redemptive grace of Yahweh that the writer selected this particular story around these particular themes? Ruth certainly stands in marked contrast to the stern and legalistic adherence to codes of law which takes the law of God outside the context of the covenant of God, and reduces a living faith to a cold moralism.

Or was the book of Ruth simply the retelling in a story of great beauty the events surrounding the bereavement of Naomi and the marriage of Ruth, perhaps to encourage virtues like love and fidelity in family relationships?

We do not know our author's exact purpose. But what is clear is that through the insights we are given into rural life in twelfth- and eleventh-century BC Palestine, the everyday routines of life, the need to work, the joys of the family, the pains of bereavement, the parting from relatives, relationships with the mother-in-law, and from the

[59] Dt. 23:3.

illustration we are given of purity, innocence, faithfulness and loyalty, duty and love, the writer is wanting his readers to discern the hand of a God who cares, sustains and provides.

We have spent much time noting that the story is set in the times of the judges. It is as though the author wished us to know that there was another side to the life of the times when the judges ruled. Certainly there were the great charismatic leaders of Judges 4 – 16, with their spasmodic successes and their basic failure to give stability and security to God's people. Equally there was the apostasy, violence, immorality and civil strife of Judges 17 – 21. But there was also faith: living faith in the gracious providence of God, which was enriching and satisfying. Perhaps the author tells the tale in the way he does to throw that fact into sharp relief – and to rekindle that sort of faith in his readers.

With such faith, our author holds to a value on human life as precious to God and to others; to an understanding of the purposes of God in his world which transcends the barriers of race; to a delight in the involvement of the Almighty with the concerns of a very ordinary family as they pray for their daily bread.

As we seek to follow the author's faith in God's providence, and discover the second story – the divine perspective – which permeates his telling of the human tale, we can learn in our day, when many are fearful of 'the evening and the dark', that the God of Israel is willing to be known as our God. Living as we do this side of Calvary and the empty tomb, with our knowledge of the incarnate and ascended Lord, we can give a fuller meaning to the phrase 'Kinsman-Redeemer' than ever Naomi, Ruth or Boaz could have understood. But we, in our way, can share with them the knowledge that 'under his wings', in the pains and joys of our ordinariness, may be found the security of his 'refuge'.[60]

[60] Ru. 2:12.

The enshrouding blackness
engulfs my being.
Alone.
Afraid.
My mind a whirlpool
ever inwards
towards an eternity of intolerable pain.

I used to reach out
a hand
into the black unknown
in hope.
But my soul was torn from me,
and I hoped no more.

It was like a pit.
Unfathomable depth.
Tortuous grovelling.
My tears the only sound
in the impenetrable darkness.

I remember that pit,
and the fear,
and the hopelessness
of an eternal agony of mind,
and the soulless wandering
in uncharted desert.

Now I find myself at this oasis,
this unlooked-for harbour,
this refuge.
I did not deserve that gracious act
to pluck me from that all-powerful deep.

I had no hope,
but turning back along the path I came,
I see a gracious hand
and a loving smile.
I see a guiding light
and feel a protecting wing.

Nestling in your warmth,
my cold heart has thawed.
The blackness of my soul
has blossomed into a million blooms.

My tears have turned to jewels,
and my bitterness to honey.

But I remember the pit.
Keep me, O Lord,
Safe
in the refuge of your wings.

Elizabeth

PART I
THE TEARS

1:1–7
1. Going away

Concern with the ordinary (1:1)

In the days when the judges ruled . . . a certain man.

In a world dominated – if we are to believe the media – by 'crisis' and 'challenge', in which every small event can be turned into a headline provided there is a 'newsworthy story' in it – and even in a church in which the unusual and the spectacular are hailed by some as more authentic than the humdrum and the routine – it is a relief to open the book of Ruth. We have already described the pleasing homeliness of its concerns: its village life, its joys and sorrows, its 'kindly virtues', and especially its concentration on the characters around whom the story is woven. This stands out all the more pointedly by contrast with the book of Judges, with which the opening words forge a connection. Judges ends with a reference to the social chaos and personal misery resulting from lack of righteous authority among the people: 'In those days there was no king in Israel: every man did what was right in his own eyes.'[1] The book of Judges is painted on a broad canvas. Although individual people feature in the book, they do so in the context of civil strife, of national upheavals, of international concerns. The book of Ruth, however, although not ultimately unmindful of the national – even global – significance of its characters, nevertheless homes in on *a certain man,* his family and their fortunes. It reminds us that the God of the nations is also concerned about the ordinariness of 'a certain man'.

Our Lord, who taught us to pray to 'our Father in heaven', and to lift our hearts and minds to the global vision of the coming of his kingdom – for his is the kingdom and the power and the glory for ever

---

[1] Jdg. 21:25.

– taught us also to pray for our daily bread. God, who knows when a sparrow falls to the ground, and who notices the gift of a cup of cold water to someone in need,[2] is concerned about our ordinariness. As Helmut Thielicke pointedly puts it:

> Tell me how lofty God is for you, and I'll tell you how little he means to you. That could be a theological axiom. The lofty God has been lofted right out of my private life.... If God has no significance for the tiny mosaic pieces of my little life, and for the things that concern *me*, then he doesn't concern me *at all*.[3]

God's interest in the fortunes of *a certain man* in the days when the judges ruled should remind us that even *our* small ordinariness is not insignificant to God, and falls within his almighty care.

The famine (1:1)

In the days when the judges ruled there was a famine in the land, and a certain man of Bethlehem in Judah went to sojourn in the country of Moab, he and his wife and his two sons.

Moving house is not a task most people undertake lightly. It is costly and unsettling. It means pulling up roots, leaving friends and neighbours. It often leads to the hunt for a new home, finding one's way in a new neighbourhood, getting to know new people. For a family it is a major upheaval. Although Elimelech would not have had the same amount of domestic gadgetry to carry with him as many a modern-day house-owner, it was not for him any less of a major decision. He decided to leave Bethlehem because of the *famine*.

Bethlehem in Judah was a large town about five miles south of present-day Jerusalem. Its name means 'House of Bread', a name which points to the unusual fertility of that area for grain harvesting (as chapter 2 of the book of Ruth makes clear). It points also to the unusualness of famine. Some commentators believe that the local famine in the Bethlehem area – apparently there was no such difficulty fifty miles to the south-east in Moab, across what we now call the Dead Sea – was due in part to the ravages associated with the chaotic times of the judges. The Midianite invasion about the time of Gideon, for example,[4] destroyed produce as well as cattle.

[2] Mt. 10:29, 42.
[3] H. Thielicke, *I Believe* (ET, Collins, 1969), pp. 33f.
[4] Jdg. 6:3f.

32

Because of the famine, Elimelech decided that he and his family should go and live for a while as resident aliens (*sojourn*) in the land of Moab.

It is not clear what prompted Elimelech to go. Whereas Canaanite religion sought to control the processes of nature with their fertility rites, the people of Yahweh were taught to trust him for blessing in prosperity on the land. Was the famine, in Elimelech's mind, a mark of God's displeasure?[5] We do not know. We do know that other Bethlehemites stayed to see the famine through and, it would seem, fared much better than Elimelech (verse 6). In the light of subsequent events, we may well wonder whether the author does not wish us to understand that Elimelech was unwise to move! Certainly the journey did not achieve its goal – to escape death. All three men of the family died in Moab. Further, by moving, they died in a foreign land, leaving Naomi the widow far more bereft and isolated than if they had remained in the fellowship of their home town.

And of all places, why go to *Moab*!

Centred on the high plateau east of the Dead Sea, Moab was populated by the descendants of Lot.[6] Though the Moabites were not attacked by the Israelites on their return to the promised land after the exodus, despite their characteristic unfriendliness, Moabites were not to be admitted to the congregation of Israel.[7] Why? They were worshippers of Chemosh, a god to whom human sacrifice was apparently made. The Moabites were sometimes referred to as 'the people of Chemosh'.[8] Furthermore, during the early period of the times of the judges, Eglon, the king of Moab, had invaded the land of the Israelites and pressed the people of Israel into servitude for eighteen years.[9] It was therefore a very curious place for the worshipper of Yahweh from Bethlehem to choose for his sojourn. Why did they not go somewhere where Yahweh was worshipped? Was this distrust in the providence of God? While commending Elimelech's desire, as he assumes, to care for his family in their hunger, Matthew Henry asks how the move to Moab could possibly have been justified. 'It is evidence of a discontented, distrustful, unstable spirit to be weary of the place in which God has set us, and to be leaving it immediately, whenever we meet with any uneasiness or inconvenience in it.'[10]

We are not told enough to know whether Elimelech's action justified

---

[5] Sometimes famine is associated in the Old Testament with a specific judgment of God; cf. Lv. 26:14–20.

[6] Gn. 19:37.   [7] Dt. 2:9; Jdg. 11:17, *etc.*; Dt. 23:3–6.

[8] 2 Ki. 3:27; Nu. 21:29.   [9] Jdg. 3:12–30.

[10] *Matthew Henry's Commentary* (1708–10), *ad loc.*

Matthew Henry's comment. But whatever lack of faith or expression of discontent with Yahweh Elimelech's action implies, the rest of the book of Ruth amply demonstrates that God's gracious providence is not bound by man's foolishness. The ultimate joy in the family and purpose in their history which derive from the arrival of Ruth on the scene demonstrate the rich lovingkindness of God's providential care. It is evidence of his love that such benefits were reaped as a result of such foolish conduct. Fortunately God's providence covers even our mistakes!

The names (1:2–5)

The name of the man was Elimelech and the name of his wife Naomi, and the names of his two sons were Mahlon and Chilion; they were Ephrathites from Bethlehem in Judah. They went into the country of Moab and remained there. ³But Elimelech, the husband of Naomi, died, and she was left with her two sons. ⁴These took Moabite wives; the name of the one was Orpah and the name of the other Ruth. They lived there about ten years; ⁵and both Mahlon and Chilion died, so that the woman was bereft of her two sons and her husband.

To our author, *names* are significant. There are some characters in the book whose names we are not told, such as the important 'next of kin' who features in Ruth 4:1. So we must assume that when the writer tells us names, they carry a special significance in his purpose. To the Hebrew way of thinking, to know a person's name is to know his character, to know him. The name is the person. When Abram becomes a new person, he receives a new name.[11] When a person's name is destroyed or cut off the person is extinguished from human memory, is as though he had never been.[12] It was a terrible thing to be left with neither name nor remnant.[13] Supremely when God tells his name, he tells his character, and shares himself with those to whom he speaks.[14] 'Yahweh' is his personal name, the name of the covenant God.

Elimelech means 'My God is King'. Some commentators, like Henry whom we quoted earlier, wonder if there is not some rebuke implied in telling us this name. Should such a name not express trust and confidence in God? We may certainly remind ourselves that for all for whom 'My God is King', while there is no promise of a trouble-free life, there is always the promise of daily bread, and the assurance that there is no need to be morbidly anxious about tomorrow.[15] Part of the

---

[11] Gn. 17:4–5.   [12] Dt. 7:24; Jos. 7:9.   [13] 2 Sa. 14:7.
[14] Ex. 6:2ff.   [15] *Cf*. Mt. 6:25–33.

meaning of faith may be expressed by saying that faith is what God gives us to help us cope with uncertainties. Did Elimelech live up to his name?

The name *Naomi* means 'pleasant, lovely, delightful', and the poignant significance of this name comes into prominence after Naomi's later return from Moab with Ruth her daughter-in-law, saddened by the bitter experiences which she believed she had received from the Lord's hand. 'Do not call me Naomi', she tells the neighbours, 'call me Mara, for the Almighty has dealt very bitterly with me' (1:20).

Mahlon and *Chilion,* Naomi's sons, apparently had old Canaanite names, but they are mentioned here because of their significance in setting the scene for the tears and pain of the rest of Ruth 1. 'Mahlon' seems to be linked to a root meaning 'to be sick', and 'Chilion' signifies something like 'failing', or 'pining', even 'annihilation'.

Orpah and *Ruth* are Moabite names, and their meanings are not too clear. But what is clear is their nationality. The sons of Elimelech are marrying worshippers of Chemosh, and although such marriage was apparently not forbidden,[16] Moabites were not admitted to the worshipping congregation.[17]

The family, we are told, were *Ephrathites*. Ephrath is a word often associated with Bethlehem, but it is very uncertain what it means. Places where it is used suggest that there was a special dignity or importance linked to being an Ephrathite. Its mention here possibly indicates that we are meeting a well-established family. Certainly when Naomi returned she was not a nobody (1:19). Maybe, as Leon Morris suggests,[18] her family were local 'aristocracy', a family which, when they left for Moab, were known as wealthy people ('I went away full,' 1:21). But wealth and prestige are no guarantee of material happiness or freedom from personal distress. The family is distressed enough by the famine to forsake their home for Moab. Then to the loss of material comfort and the security of home is added the pain not of one bereavement but of three. Naomi, on whom this first chapter of Ruth concentrates our attention, was alone, without home, husband, sons, fellowship, or hope of inheritance. What did the worship of Yahweh mean to her now?

---

[16] Dt. 7:3 refers only to the prohibition of marriage between Israelites and Canaanites together with other inhabitants of Canaan.

[17] Dt. 23:3.   [18] Morris, p. 249.

The deaths (1:3–5)

Elimelech . . . died . . . both Mahlon and Chilion died, so that the woman was bereft of her two sons and her husband.

Death is in one sense the most natural and yet in another the most unnatural of events. All men are mortal;[19] man's time on earth is limited. Death inescapably reminds man of his frailty and his limits – limits of which (the psalmist tells us) the Lord is not unmindful, and which are part of the meaning of his compassion for his people: 'As a father pities his children, so the Lord pities those who fear him. For he knows our frame; he remembers that we are dust.'[20] Along with all 'nature', death is part of the course of things. And yet a persistent horror, even revulsion, at death, has dominated man's thinking from the earliest times. And some contemporary funeral parlours suggest a refusal even to believe that it is real.

What significance, we may wonder, did the believer in Yahweh place on death when Naomi *was bereft of her two sons and her husband?* They were unaware of the transformation in the meaning of death which the New Testament brings. They had much less ground than we do for belief in life beyond the grave. They could not have understood the fullness of meaning in Paul's words about death having 'lost its sting', or in his description of death as merely 'falling asleep'.[21] Yet we must not forget David's confidence that he would be with his dead infant,[22] nor the very positive thinking of Psalms 49 and 73. Even for an Old Testament man of faith, to die was to 'sleep with his fathers', to be 'gathered to his people'.[23] And the despair expressed in passages like Psalm 88 is from one who believed himself alienated from God's compassion and dying under his wrath, not from a believer fully confident of God's grace.

But it is the resurrection of Jesus Christ from the dead which fills out belief into what for the Christian is now a certainty: that for the believer, death brings unending fellowship with the Lord.[24] Death for the Christian is 'setting sail for another shore'.[25] Our bodies are resurrected to more complete spiritual bodies, fitted for the life of heaven, with richer heavenly counterparts to the physical bodies which are appropriate for this world of space and time.[26] Christian hope looks forward to that 'great multitude which no man could

[19] As the writer of Gn. 3:19, 22 affirms.
[20] Ps. 103:13f.   [21] 1 Cor. 15:55; 1 Thes. 4:14.   [22] 2 Sa. 12:23.
[23] 1 Ki. 2:10, *etc.*; Gn. 25:8; Dt. 32:50, *etc.*
[24] 1 Thes. 4:17.   [25] *Cf.* 2 Tim. 4:6.   [26] 1 Cor. 15:42ff.

number', whose robes have been made 'white in the blood of the Lamb', standing 'before the throne of God to serve him day and night within his temple'.[27]

Some parts of the Old Testament do carry hints pointing towards these affirmations of faith. Isaiah, in a section which may be the basis for belief about personal destiny, as well as for national fortune, speaks of the time when the Lord 'will swallow up death for ever, and the Lord God will wipe away tears from all faces'. He then affirms that 'the dead shall live, their bodies shall rise. O dwellers in the dust, awake and sing for joy!'[28] And in Daniel's apocalyptic visions, stretching forward in faith to what he could perhaps only dimly grasp: 'Many of those who sleep in the dust of the earth shall awake, some to everlasting life, and some to shame and everlasting contempt.'[29]

But for the most part, death in the Old Testament is an ambiguous and shadowy state. On the one hand, the dead are sometimes seen as those who are cut off from Yahweh's sphere of influence. Death for them means the ending of a conscious relationship with God; Yahweh's praises are heard no more. Death is the king of terrors.[30] The shadowy underworld of Sheol, the place of the dead, is a place that is defiled and which emphasizes death's hideousness. The believer in Yahweh is not to attempt to reach those who have died, nor is he, like the surrounding Canaanites, to indulge in death rituals, like cutting his hair or his flesh as a recognition of death's power.[31] The people of Moab amongst whom Naomi now sojourned may possibly have had attitudes to death which were intolerable to the believer in Yahweh (indicated, perhaps, by the way Amos was to denounce them for 'burning to lime the bones of the king of Edom'[32]).

On the other hand, there is also in the Old Testament a strong faith that Yahweh is Lord, and Lord of life.[33] No other sovereign can rule the realm of death. So into this vacuum, faith in Yahweh stretches out feelers of hope. The psalmist at the very edge of death cries to Yahweh to remember him; and elsewhere the poet expresses the certainty that God will receive him through death into another life.[34] Or again, even if he makes his bed in Sheol, 'thou art there'. The Lord will not give him up.[35] There is a sense in which, at the point of death, Yahweh will 'snatch away' the believer to fellowship with him.[36] God himself is present to the believer in life and in death, and will not abandon him to the rule of Sheol.

[27] Rev. 7:9, 14f.   [28] Is. 25:8; 26:19.   [29] Dn. 12:2.
[30] Ps. 88:5; Jb. 18:14.   [31] Lv. 19:26–28; 21:5.   [32] Am. 2:1.
[33] H. A. Wolff, *Anthropology of the Old Testament* (SCM Press, 1974), p. 107.
[34] Pss. 88:12–13; 73:24.   [35] Pss. 139:8; 16:10.   [36] Ps. 49:15.

How much of this growing faith Naomi shared we do not know. Perhaps she had glimpsed something of the truth which is filled out for us fully in the New Testament – that for the one who comes to faith in God, death in one sense is already behind him. Christian believers are 'baptized into Christ's death'[37] and though their bodily death must still take place because the age of full glory is yet to be revealed,[38] their unending fellowship with their Lord is secure.

But however much or little Naomi herself had come to realize about the meaning of death for the believer in Yahweh, there were two aspects to her own circumstances which are clear. First, her husband and sons had *died* before their time. How well we can all identify with the Old Testament's sorrow when faced with what those who remain can only see as premature death. Abraham died in a good old age, an old man and full of years. There is a fulfilment in a life like that, like also that of Job, who sees children, grandchildren and even great-grandchildren.[39] But the death of a young person has a note of tragedy about it: 'In the prime of my life must I go through the gates of death and be robbed of the rest of my years?'[40] Hagar, the mother, laments over the impending death of her boy: 'Let me not look upon the death of the child,' and David suffers with his dying son.[41] For Mahlon and Chilion certainly, and we may assume for Elimelech also, death has come early in life; they have been 'robbed' of the rest of their years. And Naomi is *bereft* so early in her life *of her two sons and her husband.*

Secondly, although the book of Ruth gives only a faint glimpse of faith that death is not the end of fellowship (1:17), there was one certainty. The name of the man must not be forgotten. His name would live on in his inheritance. How important for him, then, that he should have a son (4:5, 10). How devastating, therefore, for Naomi that not only has she lost the three men of her household, but there is no heir by which their names will be continued and their inheritance guaranteed. Her men had died, and so had their names!

The author is here piling up one disaster on another in Naomi's life, giving us his readers a real sense of shock that one person should be called on to suffer so much. Surely it was undeserved; surely unexpected. Are we not introduced here to the dark side of God's providence – that some of our pains seem unbearable; some of our circumstances so unjust; some of our questions stay without answers?

Faith, we are to learn from Naomi, sometimes means a willingness

---

[37] Rom. 6:3; Col. 2:12.

[38] A. Richardson (ed.), *A Theological Word Book of the Bible* (SCM Press, 1957), p. 60.

[39] Gn. 25:8; Jb. 42:16.   [40] Is. 38:10 NIV.

[41] Gn. 21:16; 2 Sa. 12:16ff. *Cf.* Wolff, *Anthropology of the Old Testament.*

to leave such questions in the mystery of God, in the confidence that in
the brighter days he has shown himself trustworthy.

The Lord visits (1:6–7)

*Then she started with her daughters-in-law to return from the country of
Moab, for she had heard in the country of Moab that the Lord had visited his
people and given them food. ⁷So she set out from the place where she was, with
her two daughters-in-law, and they went on the way to return to the land of
Judah.*

Our memory keeps alive in the present the significance of past
experiences. How often the people of God are urged to 'remember' the
way God has helped them in the past. After the exodus from Egypt on
Passover night, Moses' first word to the people is 'Remember this
day . . . for by strength of hand the Lord brought you out.' They are to
remember their time as slaves in Egypt as an incentive to keep the
sabbath holy; they are to remember the Lord their God. At times of
fear, they are to remember the Lord's power. When they rest in his
blessings, they are to remember that they have also provoked him to
wrath. The basis of much of their ethical concern for their society is
rooted in their remembrance of their time as slaves, and God's rescue.
Disaster struck during the days of the judges, when as soon as Gideon
died, the people turned again to Baal, and did not *remember* the Lord
their God.[42]

But Naomi remembered. Lines of communication have been kept
open with the people at home. From Ruth's later testimony we see she
has been a clear witness to Yahweh in Moab. She has kept alive in her
consciousness the reality of the Lord's help to her people in the past.
She waited for news of his help in the present. Like the psalmist, when
consumed with grief and depression, no doubt Naomi would console
herself by 'calling to mind the deeds of the Lord'. Like Jonah in his
unenviable aquatic state, Naomi's mind was not far from prayer
('When my soul fainted within me, I remembered the Lord; and my
prayer came to thee').[43] In the hard times, faith will sometimes mean
leaving unanswered difficulties in the hands of God. Such faith will be
strengthened by keeping in the front of our minds the ways God has
helped us in the past. Peter urges his Christian readers to keep in mind
the gracious promises and gifts of God, and arouses them by way of
reminder.[44] And supremely are we bidden to recall, to rest upon and to

---

[42] Ex. 13:3; Dt. 5:15; 8:2, 18; 7:18; 9:7; 15:15; 16:12; 24:18, 22; Jdg. 8:34.
[43] Ps. 77:3, 11; Jon. 2:7.   [44] 2 Pet. 3:1.

be nourished by the saving grace of God in Christ every time we eat the bread or drink the cup of the Lord 'in remembrance' of him.[45] Faith is a journey of trust and growth; it is a moving mobile, not a still life. And when some parts swing for a time in the shadow, we trust that they will again emerge into the light as they have many times before. Part of the spirituality of the men and women of faith of Naomi's day was to meditate on the great acts of God in the past, and we can learn from them how to keep faith alive in the dark times.

So Naomi's heart has remained in Judah, and she has not allowed herself to forget her God. Indeed her ears are alert to the news which reaches her in Moab that Yahweh has not abandoned his people: the famine is over, *the Lord has visited his people and given them food.*

The Lord, as we have said, renders the name of God, Yahweh. He is the God whose personal name indicates his character: the God who is the actively existing one, the God who comes to meet his people in need, the God who sets his people free by the action of a redeemer (goel).[46] It is by the character of this Lord, revealed to her people generations before, that Naomi now measures the bitterness of her bereavement and her isolation (1:13, 21). It is this Lord who, we are told later, is worshipped by Boaz and his harvesters, and whose blessing is invoked on Ruth (2:4, 12). It is this Lord who is blessed by Naomi for Boaz' gracious generosity, who is seen as the giver of life, and under whose providential care Naomi ultimately finds joy (2:20; 4:13–14). The book of Ruth is rich in its revelation of the sort of God Yahweh is.

Our author is anxious that the character of this Lord will dominate his narrative. It is as if he wants his readers to place the detailed events of his story's pains and joys within the context of the God whose character is described by 'Yahweh'.

What significance there is in the phrase *the Lord has visited*! The report Naomi had received is not expressed in terms such as 'the weather has broken', or 'there has been an upturn in the economy', or 'the threat of invasion has gone'. All of these could have been part of the chain of causes in the recovery of Bethlehem from the famine. But no, the report comes to Naomi in terms of the Lord's action. Here is a central theme in the Bible: all of life is traced directly to the hand of God. To concentrate primarily on second causes may encourage us to

[45] 1 Cor. 11:23ff.

[46] *Cf.* Ex. 6:6: 'Say therefore to the people of Israel, "I am the Lord, and I will bring you out from under the burdens of the Egyptians, and I will deliver you from their bondage, and I will *redeem* (g'l) you with an outstretched arm."'

seek to be manipulators of the system. It is concentration on the Great Cause which teaches us to live by faith.

When the Lord 'visits' his people, he does so in either judgment[47] or blessing.[48] The food now available in Bethlehem is understood by Naomi as God's gift. The sense of this is caught by the psalmist: 'I will abundantly bless her provisions; I will satisfy her poor with bread';[49] it is caught also by the priest Zechariah centuries later, as he delighted in the birth of Messiah's messenger: 'Blessed be the Lord God of Israel, for he has visited and redeemed his people.'[50] With Naomi's confidence in that God, she can handle, as we shall see, the feelings of anger towards him which her circumstances provoke.

She now sets off with Ruth and Orpah to journey home.

[47] *Cf.* Ex. 20:5; 32:34; Lv. 18:25; Dt. 5:9. *Cf.* also the sense of God's punishment in Is. 10:12; 13:11.
[48] *Cf.* Gn. 50:24; Ex. 4:31; 1 Sa. 2:21, *etc.*
[49] Ps. 132:15.   [50] Lk. 1:68.

2. Coming home

Naomi's care (1:8–9)

But Naomi said to her two daughters-in-law, 'Go, return each of you to her mother's house. May the Lord deal kindly with you, as you have dealt with the dead and with me. ⁹The Lord grant that you may find a home, each one of you in the house of her husband!' Then she kissed them, and they lifted up their voices and wept.

Real faith can always be measured by its loving fruit,[1] and Ruth, the Moabitess who comes to faith herself in Naomi's God, must have learned from Naomi the reality of faith, by experiencing its benefits in her mother-in-law's active love towards her.

Naomi is now established in the story as the main character of Ruth 1. In the unfolding of the 'second story', the theme of the providence of God in the ordering of the events of the human situations in which Naomi and her daughters-in-law find themselves, and God's subsequent provision for Ruth and for Boaz, we are to concentrate first on Naomi, and especially on Naomi's unshaken faith in Yahweh. Specifically here we see one way in which Naomi's faith showed itself active in love.[2]

Naomi's loving concern for her daughters-in-law first of all finds expression in prayer. As has been well said, 'What a man believes or does not believe about prayer is a good guide to his religious beliefs in general. What he believes about prayer is an indication of what he believes about God. More particularly, what a man *does* about prayer is an indication of what he believes about it.'[3]

---

[1] *Cf.* Mt. 7:15–20; Jas. 2:8–17.   [2] *Cf.* Gal. 5:6 NEB.

[3] P. Forster, 'Providence and Prayer', in T. F. Torrance (ed.), *Belief in Science and in Christian Life* (Handsel Press, 1980), p. 110.

Prayer is, as it were, the flip side to the doctrine of providence. Prayer is the acknowledgment, not of the psychological benefit of some mythological exercise, but of the fact that we *believe* that God is there, God cares, God rules and God provides, and believe it in such a way that we are ready to do something on that basis, namely speak to him. Providence reminds us of our creatureliness and dependence on God, and that together with all men, we stand under God's lordship; prayer is an activity by which we acknowledge that we cannot be our own lord. Providence reminds us that everything is not ultimately absurd or meaningless; prayer is our way of expressing our 'yes' to the conviction that God is working his purposes out in nature, in men, in history. Providence is a reminder that the Lord is a God of grace and generosity; prayer is our way of responding to his invitation to be a member of his covenant family, his son or daughter, his co-worker in this world. Providence reminds us that the living God is not an irresistible fate before whom we can only keep silent and passive; prayer is our response to God's invitation to share fellowship with him, an expression of our union with him. As P. Forster has put it,

> The profundity of God's lordship is such that he allows us a place in his government of the world.... This points to the seriousness of our actions as Christians. It does not mean that we hold the reins of world government. They are in the hands of God. But we have our place in their exercise. In his supreme omnipotence and omniscience God wills to share his life with us.[4]

As Forster goes on to say, God will rectify and amend our prayer in his answering of it. It is not as if our prayer is the certain and secure thing, and God's answer unsure and uncertain. It is the opposite. It is we who are challenged in prayer, not God.

By prayer, therefore, we both express our trust in God's providence, and discover how our own wills are to be more aligned with his sovereign and loving will for us. Our action in prayer is met by his transforming answer.

So it was for Naomi in her prayer for Ruth and Orpah. She prayed as one who knew her God as the covenant Lord. Her prayer here is that of trusting commitment of the future to the Lord's hands. As she thinks of her daughters-in-law, and their needs, she prays that the Lord, the covenant God would *deal kindly* with them.

[4] *Ibid.*, p. 127.

Covenant love

Kindly (verse 8) translates the great word at the centre of God's covenant relationship with his people: *ḥeseḏ*, steadfast love and faithfulness. It is a word which 'combines the warmth of God's fellowship with the security of God's faithfulness'.[5] It is the word of love for which Moses sings the praise of the redeemer,[6] and by which the people are called into covenant fellowship with him. God is praised for his *ḥeseḏ* by Naomi in 2:20, and Ruth is praised for hers in 3:10. It is thus a word which tells us something of the character of the covenant God, and also something of the people who show that character in their lives, We will come back to this word in chapter 4.

The New Testament counterpart to this word is *agapē*, describing the self-giving love of God for his people, and the love he delights they should show in return. Perhaps the closest we get to a definition is 1 John 4:10–11: 'In this is love, not that we loved God but that he loved us and sent his Son to be the expiation for our sins. Beloved, if God so loved us, we also ought to love one another.'

Naomi trusts in the God of love, and commends Ruth and Orpah to his care. Her daughters-in-law have shown wonderful kindness to her and her late family; may God show his love to them. Her particular concern for them is that they should return to their own families in Moab, where Ruth's parents at least were still apparently alive (2:11), and marry again.

A home

The Lord grant that you may find a home indicates primarily the desire for a 'place of rest'.[7] The word refers not only to the ceasing of trouble and pain – that Ruth and Orpah should be able to get over their bereavement sorrow – but to the positive experience of God's security and comfort. 'Return, O my soul, to your rest,' sings the psalmist, 'for the Lord has dealt bountifully with you.'[8]

To understand the full significance of Naomi's prayer, we need to know something of the situation of widowed women in those days. Whereas the status of women in Old Testament society was very far below that accorded in the New Testament by Jesus (in his treatments of the woman at the well, the Syro-Phoenician, Mary and Martha, as well as in his teaching concerning divorce in which he grants women

---

[5] From J. A. Motyer.   [6] Ex. 15:13: Dt. 7:9.
[7] As AV and RV render this word.   [8] Ps. 116:7.

rights equal to those of men),[9] the plight of the widow was even more unenviable. The wife was included in the husband's possessions, could be repudiated, and did not have the right of inheritance.[10] She was, though, much more than a slave, and especially when a male child was born, she was respected within the family. But her security rested with the husband and she had few rights of her own.

When her husband died, therefore, the widow – especially if she had young children to support – was in a very difficult position. The word translated 'widow' connotes not only the death of the husband but also ideas of loneliness, abandonment and helplessness.[11] The widows are often mentioned alongside orphans and strangers.[12] They are in special need of protection, and Yahweh particularly cares for them.[13] Therefore the people are called on to look after the rights of widows, and various Pentateuchal laws sought to ease their lot.[14] However, complaint about the unjust treatment which widows received is a constant theme of the prophets.[15]

The one lasting hope for some recovery of social status for the widow of marriageable age was to marry a second time. How much depth of feeling from her widowhood must Naomi have put into her prayer for the younger women, therefore: *The Lord grant that you may find a home.*

The pain of partings (1:9b–14)

Then she kissed them, and they lifted up their voices and wept. ¹⁰And they said to her, 'No, we will return with you to your people.' ¹¹But Naomi said, 'Turn back, my daughters, why will you go with me? Have I yet sons in my womb that they may become your husbands? ¹²Turn back, my daughters, go your way, for I am too old to have a husband. If I should say I have hope, even if I should have a husband this night and should bear sons, ¹³would you therefore wait till they were grown? Would you therefore refrain from marrying? No, my daughters, for it is exceedingly bitter to me for your sake that the hand of the Lord has gone forth against me.' ¹⁴Then they lifted up their voices and wept again; and Orpah kissed her mother-in-law, but Ruth clung to her.

The weeping expressed the grief, and the grief was in part the ambivalent feelings for Orpah and for Ruth of needing to choose between their love for Naomi, and their hope of motherhood in a

---

[9] Mk. 10:11–12.   [10] Ex. 20:17; Dt. 24:1ff.; Nu. 27:8.
[11] C. Brown (ed.), *Dictionary of New Testament Theology* 3 (Paternoster Press, 1980), p. 1073.
[12] Ex. 22:21–24.   [13] Dt. 10:18; Ps. 146:9.
[14] Dt. 27:19; 14:29; 24:19f.; *etc.*   [15] Is. 1:23; Ezk. 22:7; Mal. 3:5.

second marriage. Initially they both refused to go, but on Naomi's insistence Orpah was persuaded to leave. Naomi's reasoning may well have had in mind the practice of levirate marriage to which we shall give much more attention in section 5. When a man died without a male child, his brother was encouraged to act as 'levir': that is, to take the widow, in order to raise up a child for the dead man. Maybe Naomi is reminding Ruth and Orpah that there are no living brothers for Mahlon and Chilion, who could act as 'levir' in this way, and of course the girls could not expect to wait until any future sons were of marriageable age! In any case, Naomi is past child-bearing.[16]

The author is intending to paint a picture of hopelessness and despair: Naomi is stressing the complete impossibility of providing Orpah and Ruth with fathers for their children.[17] As we shall see, the situation is far from such hopelessness, for in the providence of God, and through the action of a goel (a kinsman-redeemer) Ruth is to be given both a husband and a son. But for the present, that hope is nowhere on the horizon. And Orpah is persuaded to go. She kisses Naomi goodbye (verse 14), and presumably moves back to Moab to find herself another husband there. Chilion's property passed back to Naomi (4:9).

The grief was not only that of the daughters-in-law, however. Both Naomi's own pain and her sharing in the tearing choice confronting Ruth and Orpah find expression in her cry: *'No, my daughters, for it is exceedingly bitter to me for your sake that the hand of the Lord has gone forth against me.'* We shall refer back to this when we come to Ruth 1:21, but note here that despite the pain, her thoughts are directed towards the benefit of others (*for your sake*). And despite the pain – even anger – Naomi still holds on to the fact that what she has received is somehow from the *Lord's* hands. What is impressive is the truthfulness of her life before God. There is no hiding of the feeling, no pretence that her anger is not there, no sweeping aside with either Stoic upper-lip-stiffness, nor with false affirmations that all in fact feels well. While from the perspective of her faith in God's providence all *is* well, it certainly does not feel so. Like Habakkuk's shout at God for his apparent failure to prevent the rise of the Chaldean oppressors,[18] only

---

[16] Some commentators believe that Naomi did not fully understand the meaning of the levirate, in that, had Naomi married again, her sons would not in any case have been children of Elimelech, and therefore not true brothers-in-law to Mahlon and Chilion. But it is stretching the whole sense of this paragraph to read such difficulties into it. The author's concern is Naomi's hopeless position.

[17] *Cf.* Leggett, p. 176; *cf.* also Rowley, p. 191.

[18] Hab. 1:1–3: 'O Lord, how long shall I cry for help, and thou wilt not hear? Or cry

to find eventually that even the Chaldeans were part of God's purpose of love[19] and that there were nevertheless grounds for confidence in God's strength, even his joy,[20] so Naomi here does not hide her deepest feelings from God.

Many of us have all but forgotten how to mourn. While we need to remember that the Christian faith takes the sting out of death, and that there is a place on occasions for the gentle word of compassion ('do not weep'),[21] we must not deny the pain of parting to those who are bereaved. The time will come when the Christian affirmation of hope of life in Christ becomes the reality of the new heaven and the new earth, when 'death shall be no more, neither shall there be mourning nor crying nor pain any more',[22] but there are still times this side of heaven when we will weep and lament before our sorrow is turned into joy.[23]

The Christian faith has, of course, made obsolete much of the prolonged and painful public lamenting over the dead which was customary at times in ancient Israel. Though the worshippers of Yahweh were forbidden some of the death rituals practised by the Canaanites, they still engaged in lengthy times of wailing and beating the breast after the death of a loved one.[24] Jesus' parable of the children lamenting the dead when playing at funerals[25] indicates that some of these customs prevailed to his day. But whereas much of the hopelessness in such lamentation has been transformed for the Christian by the death and resurrection of Christ,[26] there is still a very spiritual grief at the loss of a friend, and at the intrusion of death into life. Was not this why Jesus wept at the tomb of his friend?[27] In our sorrow over death, we as Christians are sustained by the hope of the resurrection of the dead. But let us not pretend that death does not hurt, and that grief may not be expressed. Sorrow is real, and sensibilities renewed by the grace of Christ may well feel hurt more deeply and be all the more readily moved to tears.

---

to thee "Violence!" and thou wilt not save? Why dost thou make me see wrongs and look upon trouble?'

[19] Hab. 1:5–6: '*I* am doing a work in your days... *I* am rousing the Chaldeans...'

[20] Hab. 3:17–19: 'Though the fig tree do not blossom, nor fruit be on the vines, the produce of the olive fail and the fields yield no food, the flock be cut off from the fold and there be no herd in the stalls, yet I will rejoice in the Lord, I will joy in the God of my salvation. God, the Lord, is my strength.'

[21] Lk. 7:13.   [22] Rev. 21:4.   [23] Jn. 16:20; *cf.* also *e.g.* Phil. 2:27.

[24] Lv. 19:28; Dt. 14:1; Is. 15:2; Na. 2:7.   [25] Mt. 11:17.

[26] *Cf. e.g.* 1 Thes. 4:13–14: '... that you may not grieve as others do who have no hope. For... through Jesus, God will bring with him those who have fallen asleep.'

[27] Jn. 11:35.

47

After the initial shock of grief in bereavement, and the short period of enforced composure for the sake of others (for example at a funeral), real mourning very naturally leads into an experience of returning to emotions which some of us have forgotten since childhood. Feelings sometimes of guilt, sometimes of anger, are coupled with a tension which longs to be released in tears. It is after passing through this important phase in which grief can be expressed and wept over, that a person can then begin to consolidate and build again for the future.[28] Too many of us have lost touch with our feelings, or have forgotten how to cry. For us it is often harder to reach that stage of rebuilding. Let these women's tears remind us of the importance of not hiding our feelings, or pretending that they are not there. The way of maturity involves learning how to express our emotions appropriately. Naomi passed through the grief to the determination to build again for a new life in the future.

Let Naomi also remind us that our deepest feelings and anxieties are not hidden from God. She deliberately brings her feelings into the open before him. Indeed, she places full responsibility for her plight on God's shoulders! She now experiences God as her enemy (whose *hand* has *gone forth against* her). His has been the hand behind the famine and the deaths first of her husband and then of her sons. Yet she holds these bitter experiences in the setting of his covenant promise, by reminding herself and her daughters-in-law of his covenant name: Yahweh, the Lord.

What does faith in Yahweh mean in times of affliction? Later we can look back on suffering and sometimes discern good that has come from it. Sometimes not. Often, we can believe, suffering confronts us as no other experience can, with the transience and frailty of our lives. Suffering, as Dr Martin Israel's book *The Pain that Heals* illustrates so poignantly, can open to us deeper dimensions of the spiritual life. Suffering – what Dr Israel calls the 'dark face' of God – can be the pathway to growth and maturity of character: pain can heal. But at the time it does not feel like that. At the time, as Naomi's experience bears witness, the essence of trust, throughout the experience of affliction, is humbly to bow beneath the *hand* of God from whom we feel the blow, in the firm belief that – despite all appearances then – it is the hand of the loving Father.

'Grant me the strength, O Lord, so to traverse the valley of death's shadow that I may emerge from the other side a better, more compas-

[28] *Cf.* Y. Spiegel, *The Grief Process* (SCM Press, 1977).

sionate person of greater use to you as a witness and to my brother as a servant.'[29]

Such a faith must have been a major influence on Ruth.

Ruth's faith (1:14b–18)

Orpah kissed her mother-in-law, but Ruth clung to her. [15]*And she said, 'See, your sister-in-law has gone back to her people and to her gods; return after your sister-in-law.'* [16]*But Ruth said, 'Entreat me not to leave you or to return from following you; for where you go I will go, and where you lodge I will lodge; your people shall be my people, and your God my God;* [17]*where you die I will die, and there will I be buried. May the Lord do so to me and more also if even death parts me from you.'* [18]*And when Naomi saw that she was determined to go with her, she said no more.*

Whereas Orpah showed her love in her obedience to Naomi's wish that she should leave her to marry again, Ruth showed her love by remaining a daughter. Ruth, we are told, *clung* to Naomi (verse 14). This verb is the word of committed faithful 'cleaving' in a deep personal relationship – such as is used of the man for his wife in the Garden.[30] It is used also of the committed faithfulness which God desires of his covenant people in response to his initiative of saving grace.[31] Ruth, the Moabitess, the former worshipper of Chemosh, is displaying a quality of life meant to be characteristic of the people of Yahweh.

Despite Naomi's appeal to Orpah's example, and the obvious appropriateness of Ruth staying with 'her people', and presumably also the worldly wisdom of a worshipper of Chemosh remaining where 'her gods' are worshipped, Ruth insists on staying with Naomi. Our author here gives us Ruth's words, her classic and beautiful affirmation of faithfulness, determination and loving commitment. Ruth wills to share Naomi's future: her travel, her home, her faith. This is a promise of committed faithfulness in life and for life. Indeed, beyond life: the members of a family shared a common burial ground, at least in early Palestine,[32] and we can presume this was common to Ruth's people also. As Leon Morris puts it, 'Ruth is determined that nothing, not even death, shall separate' her from Naomi.[33] And at the centre of this expression of love and commitment to Naomi – in journeying, in

[29] M. Israel, *The Pain that Heals* (Hodder and Stoughton, 1981), p. 92.
[30] Gn. 2:24.   [31] *Cf.* Dt. 10:20.   [32] *Cf.* Gn. 47:30.
[33] Morris, p. 261.

home, in family, in life and in death – is a commitment to share Naomi's God. While at one level it is true that Ruth may well have thought that a move to Bethlehem might have involved the need for recognition of 'Bethlehem's god';[34] at another level, her faith is clearly much deeper. Ruth is prepared to take on her lips the name of Naomi's covenant God, Yahweh, the Lord, in the firm assertion of faith in him which underlies her oath. *May the Lord do so to me and more also* would have included a gesture calling down Yahweh's punishment on her should she fail to keep her vow.

How effective must Naomi's faith have been, even in adversity, pointing to the sovereign over-ruling of Yahweh, that Ruth, through Naomi's testimony, is now able to exercise faith herself in Naomi's God, and so regard herself as one among Yahweh's covenant people. Was it precisely Naomi's faith through the uncertainties which pointed Ruth to the Lord?

How often the Lord uses the experiences of his people, especially in times of affliction and difficulty, in pointing others to himself. When Moses went to meet Jethro, his father-in-law, he told him 'all that the Lord had done to Pharaoh and to the Egyptians for Israel's sake, *all the hardship that had come upon them in the way, and how the Lord had delivered them.*' Jethro rejoiced in the gracious deliverance from God: 'Now I know that the Lord is greater than all gods.'[35]

Likewise, Paul, shut in prison under Roman guard, which he regards as part of being 'on duty'[36] for Christ, writes to his readers in Philippi: 'I want you to know, brethren, that what has happened to me has really served to advance the gospel'.[37] Through his sufferings, the church was stirred to a new devotion, and Christ was preached.

Here in our passage, the Lord is bringing Ruth to faith, surely using Naomi's experience of grace through affliction as a persuasive testimony to himself. A God who makes himself known in the valley of the shadow can be trusted in the more comfortable days as well.

Naomi or Mara? (1:19–22)

So the two of them went on until they came to Bethlehem. And when they came to Bethlehem, the whole town was stirred because of them; and the women said, 'Is this Naomi?' [20]*She said to them, 'Do not call me Naomi, call me Mara, for the Almighty has dealt very bitterly with me.* [21]*I went away full, and the Lord has brought me back empty. Why call me Naomi, when the Lord has afflicted me and the Almighty has brought calamity upon me?'*

[34] *Cf.* Naaman's belief in territorial gods, 2 Ki. 5:17.
[35] Ex. 18:8–11.   [36] Phil. 1:16 *(keimai).*   [37] Phil. 1:12–18.

²²*So Naomi returned, and Ruth the Moabitess her daughter-in-law with her, who returned from the country of Moab. And they came to Bethlehem at the beginning of barley harvest.*

When Naomi saw that Ruth was 'determined', steadfastly minded with an unshakeable resolve (1:18), she acquiesced, and the two widows journeyed together to Bethlehem. When they arrived, the men, it seems, were out harvesting the barley at the start of *harvest* time, April. But *the women* (Knox narrows them down to 'all the gossips'!) were stirred into questionings. Naomi had been away for many years. She had gone with a husband and two sons, and comes back now a widow with a widowed daughter-in-law. Maybe her appearance told the bitterness she had experienced. When the question was asked *Is this Naomi?*, the play on the meaning of her name becomes poignant: *Do not call me Naomi, that means Pleasant; rather call me Mara, for that means Bitter.'* As we noticed in 1:13, she believes the bitter experiences she has coped with were from the hand of God: *'the Almighty has dealt very bitterly with me.'*

The Almighty

This title for God (RSV) translates the Hebrew word Shaddai, often used earlier in the Pentateuch, particularly in Genesis. There is disagreement about its root meaning, some authors suggesting that most probably the etymology relates 'Shaddai' to 'mountain' in the qualitative sense of possessing durability, solidity, trustworthiness.[38] If we trace its use through the Genesis text, however, we find three references that may clarify its meaning, and guide us to Naomi's thought when she used it.

First, in Genesis 17:1 we find that God confronts the ninety-nine-year-old Abram with the promise of children, and reveals himself as 'God Almighty'. He is here the God who can transform man's helplessness into blessing, for man's good and his glory. Secondly, in Genesis 43:14, elderly Jacob in his perplexity agrees reluctantly with his distressed sons that they should return to Egypt with their young brother, back to the (hitherto) unrecognized Joseph: 'may God Almighty grant you mercy before the man.' 'Shaddai' here speaks of the hope of God's protection at a time of uncertainty. And thirdly, in Genesis 49:25, Jacob's prophecy about his sons speaks of Joseph's coming 'fruitfulness' despite all 'harassment', and attributes this to

[38] *Cf.* W. F. Albright, *From the Stone Age to Christianity* (Johns Hopkins University Press, ²1957), p. 247 and refs.

'God Almighty, who will bless you with blessings of heaven above, blessings of the deep that couches beneath, blessings of the breasts and of the womb.' After thirteen years in the pain and isolation of prison, Joseph is raised to the premiership of Egypt! Such a blessing is characteristic of Shaddai.

And it is by referring to that aspect of Yahweh's character which is described by 'Shaddai' ('the God who is at his best when man is at his worst', as J. A. Motyer once put it), that Naomi shows the framework to her faith in which she places her pain. It is as though she is saying: You can see the bitterness I have experienced: the famine, the bereavements, the questionings, the partings, the apparent hopelessness; but I know God as Shaddai, and I can leave the explanation, and even the responsibility, for this bitterness with him.

Is this a failure, on her part, to face reality? Was Naomi wrong to think this way? Was Naomi, perhaps, blaming God for the evil which has befallen her, with the sort of slick answer more appropriate for Job's unhelpful comforters than as the reflection of a mature faith? It would seem not. It seems, rather, precisely the key to the way a person of faith can learn to cope with the pain and uncertainty of much of life's tribulation. In a world where, from the human perspective, the Preacher's words ring all too true: 'I have seen everything that is done under the sun; and behold, all is vanity and a striving after wind',[39] his other word can provide the fuller context, the wider perspective within which the 'vanity' can be coped with: 'you do not know the work of God who makes everything'.[40] It is the person who knows his God as Shaddai who can read the second story: that even the apparent meaninglessness of earthly suffering is part of a pattern of providence, and can be coped with if placed within God's hands. And not only Shaddai, for the God who made himself known in that character is the God who also told his people his name: Yahweh, a name which points to his covenanted love. And Naomi knows that the Shaddai with whom she can leave her bitterness is the Yahweh who has brought her home.

The story has often been told of the preacher who used as illustration the tangled threads on the back of a tapestry, pointing out that much of this life's experience 'under the sun', in this fallen world afflicted by sin in all its different ways, seems to us very often to be a tangle of unrelated colours, loose ends, and unravellable knots. It is only when the tapestry's other side is visible that those same threads are seen to spell out 'God is Love'. We may well not see the other side, what we

[39] Ec. 1:14.   [40] Ec. 11:5.

have called the 'second story' being written alongside and around the human story which we can read sometimes so painfully. But faith is God's assurance that such another side is there, and that in his love, even the pains will have a meaning.

This is a theme illustrated elsewhere in Scripture. When the psalmist had reached despair about the prosperity of the wicked and the apparent futility of living a righteous life, so much so that his own faith seemed swallowed in calamity and doubt, he found it a 'wearisome task' to attempt to understand. 'Until I went into the sanctuary of God' – then both the wicked man and he himself are seen in a new light. He is able, despite the continuing uncertainty, to exclaim, 'Nevertheless I am continually with thee', 'for me it is good to be near God; I have made the Lord God my refuge'.[41] David also, in Psalm 30, has been in the place of 'crying' to God for help. He has experienced what he calls God's 'anger'. He cries and makes supplication to God, and discovers that even deep sorrow can itself produce joy. The overnight visitor who comes in the clothing of 'weeping' is transformed by the daylight of the morning into shouts of joy.[42]

Our Lord Jesus, also, helped his disciples to see their perplexities and their questions in a new light, and from a different perspective. When they asked Jesus 'Why?' about the suffering of the man born blind, Jesus changed their question into the other: 'To what purpose?' They were not told the efficient cause of the pain, only the final cause: 'that the works of God might be made manifest in him.'[43]

But it is in Christ's own person that the fullest revelation of this truth becomes clear. The New Testament discloses him as God's suffering servant, as the Lamb of God on whom the sins and pains of the world are laid. In Christ, and in particular in Christ's life laid down in the death of the cross, God himself is entering into and sharing the depths of this world's suffering and sin. He takes on his own shoulders the responsibility for dealing with it. In the aweful tearing apart of fellowship between the Father and the Son, focused in the Cry of Dereliction, God shows his willingness in costly grace to be known in every human separation and pain; he hears every prayer which cries, 'My God, why?' Furthermore, in amazing condescension, he invites us to place our sin and our pain on him – even, may we say, to take out our anger on him, because he can bear it. Is not this what is happening in some of those difficult 'imprecatory' psalms, when the writer gives vent to his wrath?

Frank Lake quotes Robert Leighton, Archbishop of Glasgow in the

---

[41] Ps. 73:16–28.   [42] Ps. 30:2–8.   [43] Jn. 9:2–3.

seventeenth century, who wrote to a very depressed woman, 'I bid you vent your rage into the bosom of God.' Lake then goes on, in a poignant paragraph, to say this:

> The Cross of Christ is intended to draw upon himself the righteous anger of the innocent afflicted, who could not defend themselves or retaliate sufficiently to halt the injustice at the time and who tend therefore to delay and inevitably to displace the reaction, so that other, relatively or totally innocent people suffer. Christ was crucified in order that now our anger can spend itself, obediently and in faith, hurting the one provided, the Lamb of God. Sin becomes 'not believing in Jesus', not trusting him to take it, and in taking it, take it away.[44]

We need to learn in personal and pastoral life how to apply the gospel of God's grace in Christ to deepest emotional needs. Our feelings, too, are within the scope of God's providence.

In this chapter 1 of Ruth, Naomi has shared with us her faith in God. It is a faith that has shone out in contrast to the darkness of her troubles. She has seen the Lord's hand in the restoration of blessing to Bethlehem; she has recognized his hand going out against her in the bitter experience of bereavement; she has sought his care and protection for Orpah and Ruth; she has testified to the Almighty in the pain of her return to her previous acquaintances. This is a faith and a confidence in Yahweh which shines brightly against the dark and questioning backdrop of the days when the judges ruled. This is the faith in Yahweh that brought Ruth to trust him: the faith on which subsequent chapters of our story are based.

Ruth and Boaz take the limelight in the rest of the book, but Naomi comes into Ruth 2 as the *interpreter* of events in the light of God's providence; and in Ruth 3 and 4, she is the *agent* herself of God's providential blessings to others.

---

[44] F. Lake, *Tight Corners in Pastoral Counselling* (Darton, Longman and Todd, 1981), p. 137. The contrast is primarily that of the innocent pain felt by a foetus in the womb. Not all will be comfortable with the 'primal therapy' on which much of the counselling work of the Clinical Theology movement, founded by Dr Lake, is based. But the point of the quoted paragraph is that Christ is God's provision for our deepest emotional as well as spiritual needs.

Love's as warm as tears,
   Love is tears:
Pressure within the brain,
Tension at the throat,
Deluge, weeks of rain,
Haystacks afloat,
Featureless seas between
Hedges, where once was green.

Love's as fierce as fire,
   Love is fire:
All sorts – infernal heat
Clinkered with greed and pride,
Lyric desire, sharp-sweet,
Laughing, even when desired,
And that empyreal flame
Whence all loves came.

Love's as fresh as spring,
   Love is spring:
Bird-song hung in the air,
Cool smells in a wood,
Whispering 'Dare! Dare!'
To sap, to blood,
Telling 'Ease, safety, rest,
Are good; not best.'

Love's as hard as nails,
   Love is nails:
Blunt, thick, hammered through
The medial nerve of One
Who, having made us, knew
The thing He had done,
Seeing (with all that is)
Our cross, and His.

C. S. Lewis (1898-1963)

PART II
THE WINGS OF REFUGE

2:1–13
3. Grace and gratitude

The secret (2:1)

Now Naomi had a kinsman of her husband's, a man of wealth, of the family of Elimelech, whose name was Boaz.

Whereas most detective stories keep their secret to the last page, the writer here lets us into a secret right at the start of this chapter. That he does so is a further hint as to his over-riding purpose in his book, and his concern that we shall not be in the dark about it. At this point in their history neither Naomi nor Ruth knew that within reach of their home there lived a man of considerable wealth and influence who was related to them, a kinsman of Naomi's late husband. The day in Ruth's life with which Ruth 2:1–22 is concerned is a day in which Ruth meets this man, Boaz. At the end of the day after work she tells Naomi what has happened. Only then does the true significance of her meeting become apparent to her (2:20). Not until then does Ruth realize that the meeting is no accident, but part of the caring purpose of a gracious God.

But we, the readers, are told about Boaz in this first verse. Our story-teller is preparing us with the information here for this reason: that when later Ruth meets Boaz in what seems to her to be a purely accidental way, we are in the know. Behind the apparent chances of the ordinariness of day-to-day encounters, God is expressing his providential rule and care, his covenanted grace.

Who was Boaz, and why is this information so significant for us? While the meaning of his name is unclear (it may mean something like 'quickness' or 'strength'[1]) we are nonetheless told two important

[1] Morris, p. 269.

things about him. In the first place, Boaz is *a kinsman* of Elimelech's, a member of Elimelech's family. In the second place, Boaz is *a man of wealth.* We will look at both in turn.

A kinsman

The crucial importance of Boaz' *family* link will become clearer in due course, but it is important for us to know of this relationship, since it is only because of this kinship with Naomi that Boaz fulfils the role in which he finds himself later in the story. By 'family', of course, the Old Testament means a much wider network of relationships than our concept of the modern nuclear family of mother, father and 2·4 children. The family in the Old Testament consists of all those who are united together by ties of blood, and who live together under the same roof. Thus Noah's 'family' included his wife and his sons and his daughters-in-law.[2] Jacob's family included three generations.[3] Servants and even the resident alien were included in the family, as were the widows and orphans who lived under the protection of the head of the house.[4] The family in ancient Israel stood at the centre of a series of connected relationships: to God, to Israel (the people of God as a whole), to the land.

The family was the focus for the primary covenant relationship of the people with their God. Thus, Noah's sons, and their wives (and children if there were any) were included in the covenant made with Noah.[5] When God made his covenant with Abraham, every male – including 'he that is eight days old' – was to be circumcised. Even the infants were welcomed into covenant membership on the sole ground that they were part of the family.[6] On Passover night, the lamb was provided 'for a household'.[7] All the family were made secure in the place that was marked with the blood of the lamb. God worked by families; his covenant relationship with his people was focused in family life.

The family was the basic unit of Israelite social and kinship structure. It was the basic unit also and beneficiary of Israel's system of land-tenure, because the land, ultimately owned by God, was given to families as an inheritance.[8] In Israel's understanding of itself as God's covenant people, therefore, theological, social and economic realms were all bound together with the family as their focal point. Family solidarity was thus extremely strong in ancient Israel, and members of

[2] Gn. 7:1, 7.   [3] Gn. 46:8–26.   [4] *Cf.* de Vaux, p. 20.
[5] Gn. 9:8f.   [6] Gn. 17:9–12   [7] Ex. 12:3, 21.
[8] *Cf.* C. J. H. Wright, *What Does the Lord Require?* (Shaftesbury Project, 1978).

the wider family had obligations to help and protect one another when need arose. This was seen not only in the conviction that a man's family name must be preserved in his inheritance, but also in the 'levirate' custom by which this became possible. These we shall discuss in section 5. As we shall see, the role Boaz plays later in the story derives from his being a *kinsman* – one of the family of Elimelech. As if to ensure that we do not miss the point, the fact is repeated again in verse 3.

It is perhaps worth reflecting that much of the modern Christian concern for the well-being of 'family life' has a rather different emphasis from that of Old Testament family solidarity. As J. Gladwin rightly notes,[9] we must beware of being concerned primarily to uphold certain Western middle-class cultural patterns, believing that these are necessarily a biblical model. It may be rather more important to seek in our own terms and within our own culture to find ways of reflecting the interconnectedness of family relationships with land and with society, that Old Testament Israel knew in their context under God. C. J. H. Wright has written:

> Granted, of course, that we are not a redeemed theocratic nation as Israel was, surely we can still aim to produce a society which reflects in *some* sense, the triangle of relationships within which the family was set in the Old Testament. This would mean a society in which families would enjoy a degree of economic independence based upon an equitable share in the nation's wealth; in which a family could feel some social relevance and significance in the community; in which every family had the opportunity of hearing the message of divine redemption in a culturally relevant and meaningful way, and the freedom to respond to it. Idealistic? Perhaps. But at least it is a biblical idealism that strikes one as actually more realistic than the belief that looks for a morally revitalised society simply by calling for greater family cohesion alone, without tackling the economic forces that undermine the very thing called for.[10]

We need to affirm not only the family but also the social conditions within which family cohesion is economically viable and socially worth while.

---

[9] J. Gladwin, *Happy Families!* (Grove, 1981).
[10] Wright, *What Does the Lord Require?*, p. 14.

A man of wealth

The second thing we learn about Boaz is that he was *a man of wealth*. The expression sometimes means a 'valiant' man: it is used of Gideon, the 'mighty man of valour', and of Jephthah, 'mighty warrior'.[11] Sometimes it means a man of 'substance', as in Moses' prayer for Levi, 'Bless, O Lord, his substance.'[12] Sometimes it means 'riches', a word used several times by Isaiah.[13] It also carries the sense of moral worth – indeed it is the word used by Boaz to commend Ruth in 3:11: 'All my fellow townsmen know that you are a woman of worth', or, as the Authorized Version reads, 'a virtuous woman'. In Boaz, therefore, we are introduced to a man of integrity, a man of influence, a man of means.

All these factors in Boaz' life, and above all, the fact that he was 'related within the family', a kinsman of Elimelech, will be important in the role he is to play in the continuing story of Naomi and Ruth.

'She happened to come' (2:2–3)

And Ruth the Moabitess said to Naomi, 'Let me go to the field, and glean among the ears of grain after him in whose sight I shall find favour.' And she said to her, 'Go, my daughter.' [3] So she set forth and went and gleaned in the field after the reapers; and she happened to come to the part of the field belonging to Boaz, who was of the family of Elimelech.

One of the most important features of faith in God's providence is that it teaches us that even our accidents are within his care.

The theme of chapter 2 now develops into the growing relationship between Ruth, the poor widowed girl from Moab, and Boaz, the influential man of means who was related to Naomi's late husband. Ruth, all unaware of Boaz at this stage, takes advantage of one of the generous provisions of the law of Israel, that concerning gleaning. Out of concern for the helpless, the poor and the 'sojourner', the Levitical laws required reapers in the fields at harvest time, and also husbandmen in the vineyards and olive groves, to leave a portion of the crop, including the edges of the grain fields, to be collected by the needy. The reapers were not to go back for the grain that they had missed or dropped. Thus in Leviticus 19:9–10 we are told:

When you reap the harvest of your land, you shall not reap your

[11] Jdg. 6:12; 11:1.   [12] Dt. 33:11.
[13] Is. 8:4 (the riches of Damascus); 61:6 (the riches of the Gentiles).

field to its very border, neither shall you gather the gleanings after your harvest. And you shall not strip your vineyard bare, neither shall you gather the fallen grapes of your vineyard; you shall leave them for the poor and for the sojourner: I am the Lord your God.[14]

The motive of concern for the poor and the oppressed is expressed in terms of the character of God. Again and again in this chapter 19 of Leviticus, provisions for domestic, social, cultic, economic, and personal aspects of life are given, coupled with the refrain, 'I am the Lord.' There is something about the character of the covenant God (the Lord) which is to be matched by a certain pattern of behaviour in the lives of covenant people. In this particular case, the Deuteronomist spells out the reason more fully: 'He executes justice for the fatherless and the widow, and loves the sojourner, giving him food and clothing. Love the sojourner therefore; for you were sojourners in the land of Egypt.'[15] In other words, because God is a God who rescues slaves and cares for the poor, helpless and needy, so the socio-economic laws of the land are to express this human concern also. For the land and the people belong to this covenant God, and their pattern of life is to reflect his nature. As with the principle of the Jubilee[16] and the sabbatical year, and as with the laws of tithing,[17] the belief is implicit that the land belongs ultimately to God, and that his concern for the poor and underprivileged is to find economic expression in these ways.

It poses very markedly for us the question to what extent the economic priorities of countries which share the Christian inheritance of faith are placed under a similar obligation for economic provision for the underprivileged and poorer areas of God's world. A concern for the just distribution of earth's resources is no soft option for Christian people. It is part of the meaning of belonging to the covenant people of God. The law of gleaning was one of the ways ancient Israel understood their obligations in this respect. Ruth, as a poor widow, took advantage of it.

Ruth also realized that this provision in the law was a generous provision, a mark of grace which goes beyond personal rights in property ownership. She knew that though it was mandatory for the owner to leave something for the poor, it was perfectly possible for

[14] Cf. also Lv. 23:22; Dt. 24:19.

[15] Dt. 10:18–19; cf. 24:22.

[16] Lv. 25, esp. verse 23. The Jubilee was a general emancipation, every fiftieth year, of all the inhabitants of the land, and release of property to original owners. Cf. the sabbatical year in Ex. 21:2–6.

[17] E.g. 1 Sa. 8:15, 17; Ezk. 45:13–16; etc.

unscrupulous landowners to make life difficult for the gleaner. The poor depended to a large extent on the goodwill of the owner, as Naomi's conversation with Ruth at the end of the day makes clear: 'Blessed be the man who took notice of you' (2:19). Ruth's request to Naomi recognizes this: *'Let me go to the field, and glean among the ears of grain after him in whose sight I shall find favour.'* The word 'favour' is that used of the grace of God (Noah found 'favour' in the eyes of the Lord),[18] as well as of the gracious character expressed by one person to another. Of this we shall have more to say. For the present we find Boaz being cast in the role of the gracious provider, and Ruth the needy person who is dependent on another's grace.

Ruth's gentle loyalty to her mother-in-law, one of the most appealing features of this altogether rich and good relationship, is underlined by her request to Naomi for permission to go. Naomi is very much the human moving power in the background behind the choices of Ruth in chapters 2 and 3.

Ruth, we are then told, *happened to come* to the part of the field belonging to Boaz. Or, as the delightful old Authorized Version has it, 'her hap was to light on a part of the field belonging unto Boaz.' Here we have yet another reinforcement of our author's faith in the gracious providence of God. The writer knows, and we the readers know, that this was no accidental 'hap'. What to Ruth was sheer coincidence in an unplanned set of circumstances, we understand (as did Naomi later in the day; 2:20) as part of the outworking of God's gracious care. 'He's got the whole wide world in his hands', as the song puts it. Or, in the rather more refined language of the apostle Paul, who, after extolling the mercy, the riches, the wisdom, the knowledge and the judgment of God, reminds his Christian readers in Rome that 'from him and through him and to him are all things. To him be glory for ever. Amen.'[19]

Abraham Kuyper was Prime Minister of Holland at the turn of this century. He was also a professor of theology, a journalist, author and art lover. He founded the Free University of Amsterdam in 1880, and in his inaugural lecture included these famous words: 'There is not an inch in the whole area of human existence of which Christ, the sovereign of all, does not cry, "It is Mine."'[20] It was Kuyper's concern to bring every sphere of life consciously under the lordship and rule of Christ. And this derived from his conviction that the whole world is 'in his hands'; that 'from him and through him and to him are all

---

[18] Gn. 6:8.   [19] Rom. 11:36.

[20] A. Kuyper, quoted in H. R. van Til, *The Calvinistic Concept of Culture* (Presbyterian and Reformed Publishing Co., 1959), p. 117.

things' — that all the events of this world's apparent chance and change are in the hands of a God who has a purpose for his world, a purpose 'which he set forth in Christ as a plan for the fullness of time, to unite all things in him, things in heaven and things on earth.'[21]

> What is before us, we know not, whether we shall live or die; but this we know, that all things are ordered and sure. Everything is ordered with unerring wisdom and unbounded love, by thee, our God, who art love. Grant us in all things to see thy hand; through Jesus Christ our Lord.[22]

Having thus spoken of God's sovereignty, however, we must rescue ourselves from the very static and deterministic view of God which sometimes accompanies such a faith. The corollary is not that we are but pawns in some divine chess game, or puppets on strings worked by some celestial puppeteer. Exactly the opposite. Both Old and New Testaments leave us with the paradox (to which we shall return) that human choices and responsibilities are very much our concerns, and that the outworking of our faith — with fear and trembling — is very much work that we do, precisely because God is at work within us 'to will and to work for his good pleasure'.[23]

Here in the story of Ruth we see clearly illustrated the truth that God's gracious providence does not over-ride human decision and human action. Rather it is Ruth's request, and Naomi's encourage-ment, Ruth's unthinking choice of the field, and Boaz' free decision to harvest his field at this time, which are the instruments in God's hand for his providential care. This view of God is far from static and deterministic; it is living, dynamic and responsive.

Perhaps some of our difficulty in holding this paradox together in our minds derives from the way in which Christian traditions, both Catholic and Protestant, have sometimes thought about grace. In both there has been a tendency to think of the grace of God rather like a force. Sometimes it is imagined as some extra power over and above human strength, some second layer to life, like the cream on the top of a bottle of milk. Sometimes grace is seen as the power of a radical surgery to cut out sin and to provide a new force within to counteract the power of original sin. And of course there is something of truth in all this. But the primary emphasis to hold on to in our understanding of grace, is that 'grace' is a *personal relationship* word. Grace above all means a 'gracious relationship' between God and us. When 'Noah

---

[21] Eph. 1:9–10.   [22] Charles Simeon (1759).   [23] Phil. 2:12–13.

found grace' in the eyes of the Lord,[24] the truth is that God graciously found Noah, and invited him to share a gracious relationship with himself. So God's grace does not 'act on us' in a forceful way to remove our freedom. Rather God's gracious relationship *creates* our freedom. And his gracious providence is expressed through the outworking in our space and time of our free human choices, decisions and responsibilities.

To be sure, that is not how it always appears. The Preacher set himself the task of understanding a divine purpose in everything, and came to the depressing and pessimistic conclusion that all is 'but a striving after wind'.[25] Life appears, as it must have done earlier to Naomi in her bitter experiences, as a tangle of unconnected threads. But faith in the gracious providence of God carries with it the certainty that those tangled threads are but the back of the tapestry, the front of which spells a message of hope and grace. Indeed grace *through* suffering and uncertainty is a theme which both Old and New Testaments underline.

Perhaps one of the most telling experiences is that of the apostle Paul's threefold prayer for healing from his 'thorn in the flesh', only to be met with the transforming answer, 'My grace is sufficient for you.' As he learned then and shared with us, God's gracious power 'tranfuses and triumphs over, and even through' human weakness.[26] This is the high peak of his letter, the vantage point from which all Paul's experiences as an apostle – including his weakness, his trials, his joys, his 'accidents' – come into focus. Here at the point of need is the gracious providence of God most clearly perceived. That is the faith which sustained the apostle in his weakness. That is the faith also which long before, and with much less clarity, Ruth came to share, and which our author is here concerned to expound. This is God's world, and even our chance 'haps' are part of his over-ruling providence.

Gratitude (2:4)

And behold, Boaz came from Bethlehem; and he said to the reapers, 'The Lord be with you!' And they answered, 'The Lord bless you.'

It is not often that the Lord is so openly acknowledged by a manager in conversation with his workforce. 'The Lord be with you' – the only time this particular greeting is found in this form, which may indicate

[24] Gn. 6:8.   [25] Ec. 1:13, 17; 2:1ff.
[26] *Cf.* P. E. Hughes, *Paul's Second Epistle to the Corinthians* (New London Commentary on the New Testament, Marshall, Morgan and Scott, 1962), on 2 Cor. 12:8–9.

that it is more than mere convention – brings an awareness that even the ordinariness of daily work is seen by Boaz and his men in the context of faith in the covenant God whose land it is. There is a warmth, even a thankfulness, about the greeting. As Cooke comments: 'A religious spirit governs the relations between employer and employed on this estate.'[27]

There is a similar blessing referred to at the end of Psalm 129: 'The blessing of the Lord be upon you! We bless you in the name of the Lord!' This is very similar again to the priestly blessing of Numbers 6:24: 'The Lord bless you and keep you; The Lord make his face to shine upon you, and be gracious to you; The Lord lift up his countenance upon you, and give you peace.' It probably reflects the way the priest dismissed his congregation after worship. But the psalm uses the blessing only in contrast to a malediction. More than once the psalmist uses harvest language in doing so, and incidentally illustrates the fact that shared blessing was part of Israel's harvest ideology. The malediction against 'all who hate Zion' expresses the brevity and fragility of life in terms of being 'like the grass on the housetops, which withers before it grows up'. Then it describes economic failure by saying that 'the reaper does not fill his hand or the binder of sheaves his bosom'. When we come to the concluding verse, therefore, speaking of the absence of a work fellowship in which such blessing as we have mentioned is shared, we can presume that here also we have reference to a harvest theme. The fellowship of shared blessing is part of Israel's understanding of harvest.

Not only so, but the blessing which is appropriate for worship is appropriate also for the work place. Boaz' exchange of blessing with his workforce is very similar to that exchanged at the end of worship. There is no separation in the Old Testament between the 'sacred' and the 'secular': the whole of life is lived as 'before the face of God'. So Psalm 129 comes to its conclusion by contrasting the silence of Israel's would-be destroyers with what Maclaren calls the 'lovely little picture of a harvest field, where passers-by shout their good wishes to the glad toilers, and are answered by these with like salutations.'[28] 'The blessing of the Lord be upon you! We bless you in the name of the Lord!' Such is the picture here in Ruth 2 also: the joy of work, and the invocation of the Lord's blessing on the fruit of hard labour.

There is an acknowledgment implicit here of an essential, though mature (not childish) dependence on God. At the level of the natural

[27] Cooke, *ad loc.*

[28] A. Maclaren, *Psalms* 3 (*Expositor's Bible*, 1908), p. 334.

order, the understanding of God as Creator carries with it an understanding of the world as *contingent* – that is, he could have made it different, and as it now is, it depends on him entirely for what it continues to be – its existence and its order. As T. F. Torrance, S. Jaki and others have argued,[29] this is a basic assumption of all experimental scientific work. If the order of the universe were a logically *necessary* order, we could discover it by thinking about it from an armchair. In that its order is *contingent,* we can discover nature's patterns only by experiment. And yet science also assumes that the universe is ordered and not chaotic. A Christian responds by saying that both its order and its contingence derive from the rationality of the Creator, who in lordly freedom has given this world a limited freedom in dependence on him. And this applies at the personal as well as the impersonal level. We are moral and rational beings whose lives in all respects reflect the limits of our humanness as creatures dependent on the Creator, and also a limited freedom to respond to him in gratitude and worship, or ignore him in supposed autonomy. It is by gratitude and worship that the richness of true human freedom within God's limits is enjoyed, and become the basis for our own human creativity in love.

The psychoanalyst Melanie Klein has written much about the interaction of a sense of 'trust in good personal objects' with the capacity to express gratitude, and then of the close link between gratitude and generosity.[30] Indeed, she argues persuasively that it is the cultivation of an attitude of gratitude (such as Christians often ritually reinforce, she suggests, through such habits as grace before meals) which can mitigate the destructive impulses within us of envy and greed. An acknowledgment of dependence and of gratitude plays no small part in our emotional lives in releasing us from the crippling effects of envy and persecutory anxiety, and in liberating our capacities for generosity and creativity. For Mrs Klein, such trust is predominantly related to the infant's trust in its mother, and to the emotional maturing which such a relationship can enable.[31] How much more can – and should – the acknowledgment of dependence on and therefore gratitude towards the covenant God lead to responses of generosity in a person's relationship with others. Such was certainly the case with Boaz.

---

[29] *Cf.* T. F. Torrance, *Divine and Contingent Order* (OUP, 1981), and refs.

[30] M. Klein, *Envy and Gratitude* (Hogarth Press, collected 1975), pp. 187f.

[31] *Cf.* D. W. Winnicott's reference to 'good enough' mothering in *The Maturational Processes and the Facilitating Environment* (Hogarth Press, collected 1976), p. 56.

The Moabite maiden: 'I am a foreigner' (2:5–13)

Then Boaz said to his servant who was in charge of the reapers, 'Whose maiden is this?' [6]*And the servant who was in charge of the reapers answered, 'It is the Moabite maiden, who came back with Naomi from the country of Moab.* [7]*She said, "Pray, let me glean and gather among the sheaves after the reapers." So she came, and she has continued from early morning until now, without resting even for a moment.'*

[8]*Then Boaz said to Ruth, 'Now, listen, my daughter, do not go to glean in another field or leave this one, but keep close to my maidens.* [9]*Let your eyes be upon the field which they are reaping, and go after them. Have I not charged the young men not to molest you? And when you are thirsty, go to the vessels and drink what the young men have drawn.'*

[10]*Then she fell on her face, bowing to the ground, and said to him, 'Why have I found favour in your eyes, that you should take notice of me, when I am a foreigner?'* [11]*But Boaz answered her, 'All that you have done for your mother-in-law since the death of your husband has been fully told me, and how you left your father and mother and your native land and came to a people that you did not know before.* [12]*The Lord recompense you for what you have done, and a full reward be given you by the Lord, the God of Israel, under whose wings you have come to take refuge!'* [13]*Then she said, 'You are most gracious to me, my lord, for you have comforted me and spoken kindly to your maidservant, though I am not one of your maidservants.'*

One of the purposes, it is often suggested, for which the book of Ruth was written was as a counter to the rigid tightening up of the enforcement of laws against inter-racial marriage which took place at the time of Ezra and Nehemiah. We have previously suggested, though, that Ruth may well have been written earlier than the exile, and in any case, it does not read like a polemical political tract. Be that as it may, the book does nevertheless pose some serious questions for those who think of the people of God in Old Testament times as defined by the Israelite *race* for whom the question of inter-racial marriage was subject to legal sanction. This is a common view. Ruth herself regarded herself as 'a foreigner'. A glance at some of the pentateuchal laws prohibiting marriage between Israelites and foreigners also seems to give substance to the view that the people of God are defined in racial terms. Thus in Deuteronomy 7:3 the people of God, poised to enter Canaan, are contrasted with the nations who at present occupy that land, and are told: 'You shall not make marriages with them, giving your daughters to their sons or taking their daughters for your sons.'

Does not this seem to underline a concern for racial purity among the people of God? – a principle which has been developed to such a notorious extent in the apartheid policies of South Africa in recent years. And yet this common view is a wrong view.

In an article on 'Racism and the Bible' John Austin Baker begins like this: 'When we turn to the Bible for guidance and wisdom in our problems about race, the first and most important thing we have to absorb is that the Bible has nothing whatever to say to us.'[32]

What he means by this rather bald statement is that 'race' in our terms is not a concept of which the writers of the Bible have any idea. The distinctions, indeed antagonisms, of the ancient world were not about *race* in our sense of ethnic or colour distinctions; they were about culture and tradition and religion. The only kind of discrimination which we find in the Old Testament is cultural and religious, not racial. In fact the Deuteronomic prohibition about intermarriage which we quoted a moment ago goes on to give a reason for the law: it was not a concern about race but about religion. Intermarriage is forbidden, 'for they would turn away your sons from following me, to serve other gods.'[33] Furthermore, the reasons underlying the strong line taken by Nehemiah after the exile were precisely the same: that marrying 'foreign women' would be likely – as with Solomon[34] – to entice the people of Yahweh to the worship of other gods. It is not a prohibition of inter-race marriage, it is rather a strong prohibition against inter-religious marriage. Even this prohibition was not to emphasize exclusiveness for its own sake. Ezra and Nehemiah do not go back on the universal vision of 'Deutero-Isaiah'.[35] They rather insist on a morally and religiously defined base from which such a vision of world mission can be realized.[36] The people of God are to be known by their cultural and moral and religious distinctiveness. But that is not at all a question of 'race'.

This demolishes any attempt to defend racial segregation and discrimination on the basis of a supposed biblical principle of 'racial purity'. The first principle on which all Christian discussion of the question of race must be built is that 'as far as human kind is concerned, there is only one group'.[37] To be a member of the covenant

---

[32] J. A. Baker, 'Racism and the Bible', *Crucible* (Oct.-Dec. 1980), pp. 166f.

[33] Dt. 7:4.   [34] *Cf.* 1 Ki. 11:1f.

[35] *Cf.* Is. 42:6: 'a light to the nations'.

[36] *Cf.* Ne. 10 in which domestic and civil life, relationships, stewardship and worship are all brought into line with 'God's law' – the pattern of life appropriate for covenant people.

[37] J. A. Baker, 'Racism and the Bible', p. 167. Baker continues: 'It is with this group that the universal Noahic covenant is made (Gen. 9), on the basis of a single divine law

people of Yahweh, therefore, is a matter of response in faith to his universal promise of grace, and not a matter of race or colour or ethnic background. And this has always been the pattern of Old Testament faith. With some irony, Baker comments on the 'Parthians and Medes and Elamites and the dwellers of Mesopotamia, Judaea and Cappadocia, Pontus and Asia, Phrygia and Pamphylia, Egypt and the part of Libya about Cyrene, strangers from Rome both Jews and proselytes, Cretes and Arabians' referred to in Acts 2, pointing up the fact that they were meeting together in a universal fellowship under the *old* covenant for worship in Jerusalem when the Pentecostal gift of the Holy Spirit was poured out. What united them initially was their faith in Yahweh.

And so it was with Ruth and Boaz. Though Ruth understands herself to be a 'foreigner', Boaz welcomes her as a member of the family of Yahweh, under whose wings she has *come to take refuge*.

The insistence in the New Testament gospel that the grace of Christ and the faith of the Christian transcend all racial barriers, and must be given expression in community relations,[38] is based on the fundamental conviction that God 'made from one every nation of men'.[39] The Saviour Christians proclaim is a universal Saviour who shares our common humanity. Jesus' own dialogue with the woman of Samaria whom he met at the well of Sychar[40] affirms this same point. And it is this New Testament insistence which is foreshadowed in the gracious attitude of Boaz the Bethlehemite towards Ruth, the widow from Moab.

'Why have I found favour in your eyes?' (2:10). We have already noticed how Ruth regarded herself as dependent on grace. Face to face with Boaz she again recognizes in his careful generosity the marks of grace ('favour'). Boaz had obviously already heard of the return of Naomi and Ruth to Bethlehem from Moab (verse 11). He had heard that Ruth had come to faith in Yahweh, and of her devoted service to her mother-in-law, which the news of Ruth's persistence all day at her gleaning (2:7) must have reinforced. He knew that she had given up her own family and friends, her own religion and the fellowship of her

---

about the sanctity of human life, so that whatever privileges the chosen people may later receive, the fundamental fact is that God is in an eternal covenant relationship with all human beings on the fourfold basis of creation, moral law, judgment in history, and grace.'

[38] As Paul works out in Gal. 2.

[39] Acts 17:26. NIV reads 'from one man'; JB 'from one single stock'. [40] Jn. 4.

compatriots, to stay with Naomi. Boaz knew that Ruth, like Abraham,[41] had set out from her kindred and her father's house to another land, not knowing what the future held. And he knew that this showed the depths of Ruth's new-found faith in Yahweh (2:12), a faith seen active in love.

The news that it *is the Moabite maiden who came back with Naomi* came as no surprise when Boaz asked his foreman who the new gleaning girl might be (verse 5). Boaz immediately responds with the instruction that she is to be treated with respect (verse 9). Ruth receives this initiative as a mark of grace (verse 10), another indication for her, perhaps, of the gracious providence of her new God.

But here another aspect to the meaning of grace begins to come clear. We have already spoken of the gracious relationship between a person and God which enables them to place the changes and chances of the events of this world within a new perspective – to see 'the whole wide world in his hands'. We have referred also to the grace through suffering which sustained Naomi in her bitter experiences, a grace which is sufficient, which is 'made perfect' in situations of human weakness. Here we see that grace is also very much to do with the provision of personal needs. In his gracious providence, God not only governs his world, he also sustains it, and provides for it. The psalmist worships God for his greatness not only as creator but as sustainer and provider.[42] The world is not only an ordered world (such as our understanding of creation, and the fact that the scientific enterprise is possible, both indicate); it is, as we have said, a contingent world, reminding us of our continued and continuous dependence on God's sustaining grace. God's sustenance and provision for his world are also an aspect of his grace. And his gracious provision for us often comes through the gracious generosity of others. It is Naomi later in the day (2:20) who most clearly relates the generosity of Boaz to the gracious provision of God, but perhaps even now it was beginning to dawn on Ruth. Boaz has gone out of his way to be kind: 'Don't go to another field... *keep close to my maidens* and glean with them... *when you are thirsty drink* from the water my *young men have drawn*' (2:8–9). Certainly his kind words, and offer of at least a temporary position of status in his household (*keep close to my maidens*) were a comfort to the widow from Moab. They were possibly the first sign for her of the end to the painful tunnel down which she had travelled since her bereavement so far away. They were a sign of hope.

[41] Gn. 12:1ff.   [42] Ps. 104:5–30.

Humility and responsibility

'*Pray, let me glean*'...*She fell on her face, bowing to the ground*...'*I am not one of your maidservants*' (2:7, 10, 13). If Boaz had noted in Ruth the devotion of her loyalty to Naomi, he cannot fail to have seen her humility towards him. Although, as we have said, the law required provision for the poor, Ruth does not stand on her rights in this respect. Humbly she had requested permission of the foreman in charge: *Pray, let me glean*. This humble acknowledgment of her dependence is seen also in her response to Boaz, in bowing herself to the ground, and in her later response to his prayer: 'But what am I saying when I call myself thy maiden – since I am not worthy to be compared with the least of thy maidens'.[43]

In his valuable discussion of *Human Rights: a Study in Biblical Themes*, Christopher Wright begins not with 'rights', but with 'responsibility to God', which he regards as *the* essential characteristic of what it means to be human.

> We cannot escape that responsibility, for it is not in our power as creatures. Even to try to deny it is to acknowledge its reality. Thus Cain even in his attempt to disclaim responsibility for his *brother* by the very act of answering *God* concedes his accountability to his Creator. And inseparable from that primary answerability is the fact that God holds us responsible *for* our fellows. Since we cannot escape the intrinsic fact of our human constitution, responsibility *to* God, neither can we evade its divinely imposed correlative, obligation to God *for* our fellow humans.[44]

The striking characteristics of Boaz the man of faith, and of Ruth the woman of faith, which this paragraph highlights, are their respective refusals to stand on rights (Boaz as owner, Ruth as gleaner). We are given evidence rather of their willingness humbly to express their faith in God by *caring* (Boaz for Ruth), and by grateful and humble *acceptance* of care (Ruth from Boaz). A living faith is seen sometimes in giving, sometimes in willingness gratefully to receive.

As we noted before, we must never formulate our understanding of God's sovereign providence in such a way that our human responsibility dissolves away. God's grace does not eliminate our freedom – it rather creates it. And the first premise of all morality is that the moral person

[43] A comment from Carpzor, quoted by Keil and Delitzsch.
[44] C. J. H. Wright, *Human Rights: a Study in Biblical Themes* (Grove, 1979), p. 8.

is responsible. In the Bible, responsibility is attributed to persons made as God's image, and it carries the sense of 'response' to the Creator, who holds us accountable. Our Christian understanding of human fallenness, in which sin disorders all aspects of our personality and relationships, means that a fully restored human responsibility must be linked to our full restoration as persons, as we are gradually made more like Christ. So – as with every aspect of Christian life – there is an ambiguity in the exercise of our responsibility between the 'now' of today and the 'not yet' of the coming Day of the Lord. Responsibility is therefore both an assumption and a goal. We must be alert to the debilitating effect of the sins of others and ourselves on the exercise of our responsibility, but we are not at liberty to dissolve our moral accountability away into any sort of determinism. Our whole life is under what Barth somewhere called the 'global mandate of responsible freedom'.[45] To be responsible is to live as accountable to God and as caring for others, within the limits of the freedom which is ours in this world.

And there are limits. The fact of it being a created world puts limits to our freedom. We are free as *God's* creatures, therefore such freedom is not arbitrariness. The fact of our physical, genetic and psychological make-up puts limits on our freedom; we are who we are in some senses because of who our parents were. There are limits set by others' personalities and needs: by the law of love we are bound not to exercise our freedom at the expense of anyone else's humanity. We are obliged rather to exercise it for others' greater good. The fact of sin also puts constraints on our freedom, such that we are not always able to do that which we know to be good, or even desire to do. And there are moral limits to our freedom, which mean we must sometimes say 'we may not' when technology says 'we can'. Those limits need emphasizing in our context of ecological devastation, sexual licence, nuclear-weapons proliferation and frozen human embryos.

Responsibility is learning to 'love within limits'[46] – it is responsible dialogue with the constraints that are upon us, always open to God's direction and grace, always open to the prior ethical claim on us of the needs of others. That is what the experience of faith in God meant for Boaz and Ruth. We may learn from them the importance of living that way also.

[45] *Cf.* also K. Barth, *Church Dogmatics* III/4, pp. 47f.
[46] L. Smedes, *Love Within Limits* (Lion, 1979).

The covenant Lord

'The Lord, the God of Israel, under whose wings you have come to take refuge . . . recompense you . . . reward you' (2:12–13). Yahweh, the Lord, as we have noted before, is the covenant name for the God of Israel. According to Exodus 6:2f., the significance of this name was made clear to Moses [47] when God promised, in remembrance of his covenant with Abraham, Isaac and Jacob, to rescue and 'redeem with an outstretched arm' his people then slaves in Egypt. It was Yahweh, the Lord, who, according to Exodus 19:3ff., called Moses and established his covenant with him on Sinai, a covenant in which we are given the first sense of a 'chosen people'. It was by his name Yahweh that, according to Exodus 20:1ff., God spoke the Ten Commandments, that central distillation of principles and precepts which describe both the character of God and the pattern of life appropriate for God's covenant people, which more than anything else gave moral boundaries to the people of God, and which to a greater or lesser extent is reflected in all the other laws of the Pentateuch of the Old Testament, as well as in the Sermon on the Mount and the letters of Paul, in the New.

The Sinai covenant is modelled on the sort of suzerainty treaties which were comparatively common in the ancient Middle East. When the kings of the great empires (Egypt, the Hittites, Assyria) conquered a minor kingdom, they might allow the vanquished king to retain government of his kingdom, provided that he made an oath of allegiance to the conqueror. [48] By such a suzerainty treaty, the conquered swore his allegiance to the conquering 'great king'. This terminology has passed into the Israelite recording of their covenant relationship with God. Contrasting the Sinaitic covenant with the Abrahamic covenant which preceded it and the Davidic covenant which was to follow it, G. J. Wenham writes:

> The Sinaitic covenant is not modelled on a royal grant but on a vassal treaty, a legal form in which the vassal's obligations are much more prominent. But even here the laws are set in a context of a gracious, divine initiative. Obedience to the law is not the source of blessing, but it augments a blessing already given. [49]

---

[47] Cf. also art. 'God' in A. Richardson (ed.), A Theological Word Book of the Bible (SCM Press, 1957).

[48] Cf. G. J. Wenham, 'Grace and Law in the Old Testament' in G. J. Wenham and B. N. Kaye (eds.), Law. Morality and the Bible (Inter-Varsity Press, 1978), p. 7.

[49] Ibid., p. 5.

There is a pattern, therefore, of God's choice and initiative of grace, of man's obedient response in worship and service, which in turn leads to the further enjoyment of God's further blessings.

Turning back now to the prayer of Boaz for Ruth (2:12), we can see clear evidence of Boaz' consciousness of being a member of this covenant family of the God of Israel. His knowledge of God as Yahweh, the Lord, his description of Yahweh's grace in terms of 'wings of refuge', then his recognition of Ruth's lowly and obedient response to grace seen in her devotion to Naomi, and finally his expectancy that the Lord would further bless her, all display the pattern of God's covenanted relationship with his people. 'In these words', comment Keil and Delitzsch on this verse, 'we see the genuine piety of a true Israelite.'

'Recompense' and 'reward'

Christian devotion has always rightly been chary of doing good 'for the sake of a reward'. Yet 'recompense' and 'reward' are the words Boaz uses here. We must understand Boaz' prayer for God's 'payment' back to Ruth for her devoted service in the context of his faith in the covenant Lord. The word *recompense* is used with a number of different nuances in the Old Testament. It is related to the word for 'peace'. It can have the sense of 'pay', as when Elisha told the wife of one of the prophets' sons: 'Go, sell the oil and pay your debts.'[50] It can have the sense of 'making good'. When an ox or an ass fell into an open pit which a man had dug and left uncovered, the law of the Book of the Covenant required him to 'make it good'.[51] Similarly, 'he who kills a beast shall make it good, life for life.'[52] This is the word sometimes used also for 'restore' ('I will restore to you the years which the swarming locust has eaten'[53]) and for 'making complete again', 'making peace'.[54] The word for 'reward', however, is an infrequent word in the Old Testament, occurring otherwise only in Genesis,[55] where in each case it means 'wages'.

Boaz' prayer is therefore that God should 'make up what is due' to Ruth for all the pain she has suffered in her self-giving to Naomi – may she be 'paid sufficiently' and 'restored to a sense of completeness and peace' once again.

But what are we to make of this concern for 'payments' and 'rewards'? Might not this seem to turn the concern for piety into one of a prudent regard for what one might get out of it? Does Boaz' faith

---

[50] 2 Ki. 4:7.   [51] Ex. 21:33–34.   [52] Lv. 24:18.   [53] Joel 2:25.
[54] *E.g.* 2 Sa. 10:19; 1 Ch. 19:19.   [55] Gn. 29:15; 31:7; 31:41.

point to a belief that one needs to earn God's favour by self-giving service? Is not the primary thrust of the New Testament that we are justified by grace through faith, not by works?[56] But then we recall that the New Testament also seems to have not a little to say about rewards. Jesus speaks of a 'rich reward in heaven' for those who are persecuted.[57] He teaches that the Father who sees his children giving alms, and praying and fasting in secret, will reward them.[58] Even a cup of cold water will not go unrewarded; and God is described as the 'rewarder' of those who seek him, and the one who rewards his prophets and saints.[59] What are we to make of this?

It helps, perhaps, to distinguish what have been called 'arbitrary' rewards from 'proper' rewards. Arbitrary rewards have no direct relationship to the behaviour for which they are given. There is nothing necessarily wrong in being rewarded arbitrarily (like being paid money for an oil painting you have created). There may, though, be something wrong about seeking the arbitrary reward for its own sake. This was the fault of the hypocrites who blew their trumpets and prayed at the street corners and disfigured their faces when fasting 'so that they may be seen by men'.

By contrast, 'proper' rewards are the direct and integrally related consequence of behaviour (like the satisfaction of being able to paint after hard practice). Thus the proper reward for almsgiving, prayer and fasting is the relationship with God which these activities are intended to express. So when Jesus urges that good deeds should be done without concern for reward,[60] he does also imply that the 'proper' reward for goodness can be left to God. The enjoyment of the rewards of good character, from which the fruit of good actions derive,[61] is the same as the enjoyment of God himself. An enriched relationship with God is the 'proper reward' of loving obedience to him in response to his gracious initiative of love. The Authorized Version captures the sense, if not the accurate translation, of Genesis 15:1: there is something of God himself, experienced in all his benefits.[62] His word to Abram is: 'Fear not...I am thy shield, and thy exceeding great reward.' As Calvin comments on this verse, the word 'reward' has the force of 'inheritance' or 'felicity'. He urges that we should have it deeply graven on our minds that in God alone we have the highest and complete perfection of all things, and that 'we shall be truly happy

[56] Cf. Rom. 3:24–28; 5:1, etc.   [57] Mt. 5:12.   [58] Mt. 6:4, 6. 18.
[59] Mt. 10:41; Heb. 11:6; Rev. 11:18.
[60] Lk. 14:12–14.   [61] Mt. 7:17.
[62] But see G. von Rad, Genesis (SCM Press, ²1963), p. 178.

when God is propitious to us; for he not only pours upon us the abundance of his kindness, but offers himself to us that we may enjoy him'.[63]

> Whosoever shall be fully persuaded that his life is protected by the hand of God, and that he never can be miserable while God is gracious to him; and who consequently resorts to this haven in all his cares and troubles, will find the best remedy for all evils. Not that the faithful can be entirely free from fear and care, as long as they are tossed by the tempests of contentions and of miseries; but because the storm is hushed in their own breast; and whereas the defence of God is greater than all danger, so faith triumphs over fear.[64]

Boaz' prayer for Ruth concerns her experience of an enriched relationship with God as the 'proper reward' for the loyalty to Naomi which she believed her new faith in Israel's covenant God had prompted.

The wings of refuge

Boaz' prayer concludes with this phrase which in many ways focuses the theme of the whole book. It includes this delightful picture of God as an eagle, fluttering its wings over its young. The song of Moses recorded in Deuteronomy 32:11f. uses the same imagery: 'like an eagle that stirs up its nest, that flutters over its young, spreading out its wings, catching them, bearing them on its pinions, the Lord alone did lead him.' Similar pictures are drawn in the Psalms. God's 'wings' describe a place of *safety* ('Hide me in the shadow of thy wings, from the wicked'),[65] or a place of *refreshment* ('How precious is thy steadfast love, O God! The children of men take refuge in the shadow of thy wings. They feast on the abundance of thy house, and thou givest them drink from the river of thy delights').[66] Elsewhere the picture is of a place of *stillness* in the storm ('Be merciful to me, O God, be merciful to me, for in thee my soul takes refuge; in the shadow of thy wings I will take refuge, till the storms of destruction pass by').[67] Sometimes it describes a place of *help and relaxation* ('Thou hast been my help, and in the shadow of thy wings I sing for joy').[68] Sometimes the thought is of *hope* when circumstances are otherwise full of fear ('He who dwells in the shelter of the Most High, who abides in the shadow of the Almighty, will say to

[63] J. Calvin, *Genesis* (Banner of Truth, 1965 edn.), p. 400.
[64] *Ibid.*   [65] Ps. 17:8.   [66] Ps. 36:7f.
[67] Ps. 57:1.   [68] Ps. 63:7.

the Lord, "My refuge and my fortress; my God, in whom I trust." For he will deliver you from the snare of the fowler and from the deadly pestilence; he will cover you with his pinions, and under his wings you will find refuge; his faithfulness is a shield and buckler. You will not fear...').[69] Safety, refreshment, stillness, help, relaxation, hope: these are the words associated with God's 'wings'.

There is a basic human longing for God, captured in the picture of the prodigal son far from home, and in the words of Augustine, that our hearts find no peace until they find their rest in God,[70] and in the 'evening, the dark and the fear' of some of our contemporary authors. How satisfying to the 'alienated' person, to the one who feels himself 'alone in the unfeeling immensity of the universe',[71] to find that far from the ancient covenant being 'in pieces',[72] God is there, God cares, God rules, God provides.

> O Lord our God, let the shelter of your wings give us hope. Protect us and uphold us. You will be the Support that upholds us from childhood till the hair on our heads is grey. When you are our strength we are strong, but when our strength is our own we are weak. In you our good abides for ever, and when we turn away from it we turn to evil. Let us come home at last to you, O Lord, for fear that we be lost. For in you our good abides and it has no blemish, since it is yourself. Nor do we fear that there is no home to which we can return. We fell from it; but our home is your eternity and it does not fall because we are away.[73]

May Ruth find in the God of Israel such a provision for her needs! Her predicament has been that of an isolated widow in a foreign land, and she is now apparently under continuing danger of being molested (2:22). She has been hungry, on the move, anxious, and doubtless emotionally drained. How much she needs a place of safety and refreshment. She longs to find stillness, relaxation and a new hope. It is Boaz' prayer that this will be her experience through her trust in Yahweh.

As the rest of the story unfolds, we discover that the one who prayed this prayer is in fact the one through whom it is answered! It is through Boaz himself that Ruth is given security, is provided with refreshment and nourishment, comes to a place of rest in the joy of marriage, and is

---

[69] Ps. 91:1ff.   [70] Augustine, *Confessions*, Book I/1.
[71] J. Monod, *Chance and Necessity* (ET, Collins, 1971), p. 167.
[72] *Ibid.*   [73] Augustine, *Confessions*, Book IV/16.

given the hope of a new home and a new family name. We, as the covenant people of God, the Israel who belong to Christ, can properly pray that same prayer for ourselves and for others. It is for us both to experience the refuge of his wings, and to be ready to be the means by which others may experience this also. As Helmut Thielicke puts it at the end of his great sermon on the prodigal son and the waiting father, 'There is a homecoming for us all because there is a home.'[74]

[74] H. Thielicke, *The Waiting Father* (James Clarke, 1960), p. 29.

2:14–23

4. A place in the family

'Handfuls of purpose' (2:14–16)

And at mealtime Boaz said to her, 'Come here, and eat some bread, and dip your morsel in the wine.' So she sat beside the reapers, and he passed to her parched grain; and she ate until she was satisfied, and she had some left over. ¹⁵*When she rose to glean, Boaz instructed his young men, saying, 'Let her glean even among the sheaves, and do not reproach her.* ¹⁶*And also pull out some from the bundles for her, and leave it for her to glean, and do not rebuke her.'*

There is no place for legalism in the faith of the people of God. A cold adherence to the strict letter of law takes law outside the covenant of grace, at the heart of which is a relationship of generous love, which law is intended to safeguard and, through the exercise of obedience, to deepen and enrich. These verses point not merely to sufficient provision for Ruth's needs, but like the basketsful left over after the 5,000 had fed,[1] to a generosity which gave her even more than she required. Boaz offers her freshly roasted ears of the newly picked grain *until she was satisfied, and she had some left over* – enough left over in fact to offer to Naomi when she got home (2:18). Boaz told her to glean *even among the sheaves*, whereas the law mentioned only the edges of the field. Boaz even tells his young men to 'let fall also some of the handfuls of purpose for her' (as the quaint rendering of the Authorized Version of 2:16 has it), so that there is more available for Ruth. We have commented before[2] on Boaz' generous response which goes beyond the strict requirement of law.

And yet we need to remind ourselves that in Israelite religion the law was never an external code merely requiring legalistic subservience.

[1] Jn. 6:13.   [2] See above, p. 69.

78

The law has to be understood within the covenant relationship, within the total ordering of the people's lives under their covenant God. It was the separation of law as a category distinct from the covenant relationship, particularly in the inter-testamental period, which led to the development of the legalistic approach to the Old Testament seen in the Pharisaic teaching condemned by Jesus. No, the law – certainly by the time of Deuteronomy, if not earlier – is very much part of the 'sphere of operation of the spiritual and moral life, where external compulsion must be replaced by personal moral decision'.[3] In the Deuteronomic material in particular, the primary commandment is that of love for God, and 'each individual ruling is only to be understood rightly as the will of God in so far as it is comprehended as the detailed expression of an overall injunction of love, by which God claims man for his own – not just in this or that particular obligation, but in man's whole personal being.'[4] 'These laws, which can be so easily taken in a legalistic sense as individual casuistic definitions quite unrelated to one another, are to be understood as the application and practice in particular concrete situations of the primary command of love.'[5]

What we are seeing in Boaz, therefore, is an indication of his gracious generosity which, by going beyond the letter of the law concerning gleaning, nevertheless did demonstrate the spiritual concern for which that law was framed, namely, that love for God is expressed in care and provision for the poor. By so doing Boaz is sharing something of the character of the God made known more fully to us in Christ, who, so the apostle teaches, is 'able to do far more abundantly than all that we ask or think'.[6]

'O generous love' (2:17–20a)

So she gleaned in the field until evening; then she beat out what she had gleaned, and it was about an ephah of barley. [18]*And she took it up and went into the city; she showed her mother-in-law what she had gleaned, and she also brought out and gave her what food she had left over after being satisfied.* [19]*And her mother-in-law said to her, 'Where did you glean today? And where have you worked? Blessed be the man who took notice of you.' So she told her mother-in-law with whom she had worked, and said, 'The man's name with whom I worked today is Boaz.'* [20]*And Naomi said to her daughter-in-law, 'Blessed be he by the Lord, whose kindness has not forsaken the living or the dead!'*

After her day's hard work, Ruth beat out her gleaning to leave the edible barley, and was able to take back home an enormous *ephah*

[3] Eichrodt, p. 93.   [4] *Ibid.*   [5] *Ibid.*   [6] Eph. 3:20.

(nearly five gallons – it was the name of a vessel large enough to hold a person),[7] to her mother-in-law's evident surprise and delight. Naomi prays a blessing on Ruth's benefactor, before even she knew who it was, and when Ruth then tells her that his name was Boaz, Naomi bursts forth in a prayer of thanksgiving and blessing: *'Blessed be he by the Lord, whose kindness has not forsaken the living or the dead!'* Quite why she was so exultant, and why she mentions the 'dead' (a reference in fact to her late husband Elimelech), will become clearer in a short while.

But first let us pause with the word translated 'kindness', and try to fill out a little more the meaning of the 'kindness' of the Lord to which Naomi refers. This word *ḥeseḏ* (used earlier of God in 1:8 in Naomi's prayer for Orpah and Ruth, and again in 3:10 by Boaz, this time of Ruth) is one of the words characteristic of a covenant relationship. When we read of covenants of loving commitment between people (as between David and Jonathan), the 'kind of behaviour which is expected in the normal way, of those so associated' is described by *ḥeseḏ*.[8] It is the warmth of loyal love [9] combined with 'brotherly comradeship' and a sense of committed and reliable faithfulness. This is the word very frequently used to describe God's covenanted love-faithfulness to his people.[10] As Eichrodt illustrates, the mighty redeemer from Egypt, and the law-giver of Sinai, is the loving protector who remains true to his promises. This God teaches his people about his loyalty and love[11] by keeping them through their wilderness wanderings, and by forgiving their sins.[12] Even when God punishes, he does so in order to restore a broken covenant relationship.[13]

'The unbreakable character of the divine disposition of love' is beautifully reflected in the description of outstanding human loyalty in terms of the sort of loving constancy which Yahweh both desires and demonstrates. Thus David desires to show Jonathan the 'loyal love of the Lord' and at a later stage in his life, asks whether there is 'some one

---

[7] Cf. Zc. 5:6ff.   [8] Cf. 1 Sa. 20:8; and Eichrodt, p. 232.
[9] 1 Sa. 20:14.
[10] Eichrodt goes on to contrast Yahweh's constant love for his covenant people with the superficially similar, but in fact quite different, understanding of the help of God testified in contemporary religions: 'In spite, however, of these resemblances in the picture of God, the differences which undoubtedly exist should not be forgotten. In particular it is the association of Yahweh's *ḥeseḏ* with the covenant relationship which gives the divine loving kindness an incomparably firmer basis. Because in Israel it was possible to speak of one God, whose demands sought jealously and exclusively to shape the whole of life, the succour and loving kindness of this God were given an internal foundation which will be sought in vain among the Babylonian nature deities.'
[11] Ex. 20:6; 34:6.   [12] Ex. 15:13; Nu. 14:18–20.
[13] Nu. 14:20ff.; 2 Sa. 7:14ff.

of the house of Saul, that I may show the kindness of God to him.'[14]

The frequent Old Testamant imagery of God as the Father-Shepherd of his people also draws out something of the distinctive meaning of Israel's understanding of the *hesed* of Yahweh. He is 'Father' first because he is Creator, which gives him a claim on the worship of his people, but his fatherhood is expressed in compassion and he is even known as the Father of the fatherless.[15] He is Shepherd giving his covenant people the sense of the strong security of being the 'people of his pasture, and the sheep of his hand'.[16]

The character of *hesed* is perhaps most clearly seen by Yahweh's willingness (which his people only gradually came to appreciate) to allow his love to continue in mercy towards his people, even when their sin threatened to disrupt and even destroy the covenant relationship altogether. This builds into the concept of loyal love the sense also of an undeserved mercy. Nowhere is this more richly illustrated than in the life-story of Hosea: the 'love although'[17] by which the prophet's continuing love for the adulterous woman is to parallel the faithful and merciful love of Yahweh for Israel, even though they had turned to other gods. As Eichrodt again points out, this contributed to a deepening of the father-image as applied to God. Listen to the way Hosea writes:

When Israel was a child, I loved him,
    and out of Egypt I called my son.
The more I called them,
    the more they went from me;
they kept sacrificing to the Baals,
    and burning incense to idols.
Yet it was I who taught Ephraim to walk,
    I took them up in my arms;
    but they did not know that I healed them.
I led them with cords of compassion,
    with the bands of love,
and I became to them as one
    who eases the yoke on their jaws,
    and I bent down to them and fed them.[18]

But later than Hosea, Jeremiah – says Eichrodt again – goes even further:

[14] 1 Sa. 20:14; 2 Sa. 9:3.   [15] Is. 63:15–16; Ps. 68:5.   [16] Ps. 95:7.
[17] Ho. 3:1.   [18] Ho. 11:1–4.

He sees the father-relationship as an image of undying love, the kind of love which will take the lost son to its arms again with fervent emotion, whenever that son returns in penitence; and this despite the fact that even the love itself cannot give a reason for the triumph of such compassion over the most justifiable indignation, but is aware of its own behaviour only as an inner but incomprehensible imperative.[19]

Here he is referring to Jeremiah 31:20 ('Is Ephraim my dear son? Is he my darling child? For as often as I speak against him, I do remember him still. Therefore my heart yearns for him; I will surely have mercy on him, says the Lord'). The tone of this is recalled for us in Jesus' parable recorded in Luke 15 of the waiting father and the prodigal son.

The ḥese_d which is part of the 'matter of course' of a covenanted relationship now becomes transformed into a rich gift of grace, given to men who have no claim upon it. 'The miraculous quality of this new love is seen to reside not only in the condescension of the exalted God, but also, much more inwardly, in the mystery of a divine will which seeks communion with man.'[20]

This is the character of the God whom Naomi knows as Yahweh, and to whom she has trusted herself. She perhaps did not have the fullness of understanding which we have found so eloquently expounded in the prophets. But there are large hints that even in her perhaps more limited understanding, God had nevertheless made himself known to her as a God whose gift of grace is given even to those who have no claim upon it. This ḥese_d, this merciful and gracious lovingkindness, she sees in the gracious generosity of Boaz to Ruth. Naomi's whole attitude of mind has been to see the hand of the Lord in the circumstances of her life. Earlier she had held on to his grace through the sufferings of her bereavement. Now she experiences the grace of his provision through the generosity of a wealthy farmer. We, too, can learn to see in all our circumstances the hand of a gracious God.

Agencies of grace

We must now underline the fact that Naomi sees the gracious hand of God acting through the gracious actions of men. As we saw before, so here, there is no sense that the grace and kindness of God over-ride human agency, but rather that it is often through human agency (in

---

[19] Eichrodt, p. 238.　　[20] *Ibid.*, p. 239.

this case of Boaz) that God's gracious kindness is received.

We find exactly the same pattern in one of the apostle Paul's paragraphs about grace in his second letter to Corinth. He tells his readers that he wants them to know about the grace of God, which he expounds as 'the grace of our Lord Jesus Christ, that though he was rich, yet for your sake he became poor, so that by his poverty you might become rich.'[21] But in this passage, he is talking about money! – and he goes on to teach the Corinthians about social equality.[22] The grace of God in this context is seen in the generous behaviour of the churches of Macedonia, 'for in a severe test of affliction, their abundance of joy and their extreme poverty have overflowed in a wealth of liberality on their part. For they gave according to their means, as I can testify, and beyond their means, of their own free will, begging us earnestly for the favour of taking part in the relief of the saints.'[23] He then urges the Corinthians to 'excel in this gracious work also'; 'I do not mean that others should be eased and you burdened, but that as a matter of equality your abundance at the present time should supply their want, so that their abundance may supply your want, that there may be equality.'[24]

To believe in God's grace commits us, so Paul would say, to hard work in his service for one another. And this service will include concern about equality in the distribution of resources, and therefore about the social structures and priorities which may hinder a just distribution of the rich bounty of God's earth. There is no sense, in the book of Ruth, of those in power using the underprivileged as political pawns for personal gain. No, the mood is rather that faith in the gracious provision of God is matched by a concern to express that grace in personal dealings with others, and in particular, with care for the disadvantaged. Maybe the apostle Paul would urge us to have the Brandt Report concerning aid from the rich North to the poor South open alongside the book of Ruth, when we talk about the gracious provision of God.

Karl Barth somewhere suggests that the inner meaning and purpose of our creation as human beings in the divine image is to express 'covenant fidelity' in our relationships with him and others, and that the inner meaning and purpose of the whole created order is to be the external framework for and condition of the possibility of keeping covenant. Our lives and our relationships are intended to mirror God's life and God's relationships. The ethical question for Christians always comes to its focus in this question: how, in this situation and this

[21] 2 Cor. 8:1, 9.   [22] 2 Cor. 8:14.
[23] 2 Cor. 8:2–4.   [24] 2 Cor. 8:7, 13–14.

context, am I – are we – to give expression to the character of God and his covenant of grace?

'One of our nearest kin' (2:20b–23)

Naomi also said to her, 'The man is a relative of ours, one of our nearest kin.' ²¹*And Ruth the Moabitess said, 'Besides, he said to me, "You shall keep close by my servants, till they have finished all my harvest." ²²And Naomi said to Ruth, her daughter-in-law, 'It is well, my daughter, that you go out with his maidens, lest in another field you be molested.' ²³So she kept close to the maidens of Boaz, gleaning until the end of the barley and wheat harvests; and she lived with her mother-in-law.*

We turn in the next chapter of Ruth to the meaning for our story of Naomi's words *the man is a relative of ours, one of our nearest kin*. There the whole significance of Boaz' entry on to the scene will become much clearer. For the present, the chapter ends, as did Ruth 1, with reference to the harvest. But there the tone was one of sadness, bitterness, aloneness and poverty. Now the situation is one of hope, of comfort and provision. We have found in these chapters how the faith of Naomi, and of Boaz and Ruth, has illustrated for us something of the grace of God: the grace of providence seen in God's over-ruling care of the ordinary and everyday events of life within the context of his gracious and loving purpose; the possibilities of grace through suffering, even when the outlook is bleak, and the hand of God is very hard to discern; the grace of provision, even in the mundane matters of 'daily bread'. Ruth 3 brings us face to face with the now central figure in this drama, the one through whom the grace of God is mediated for Ruth and Naomi: Boaz, the kinsman-redeemer.

Love bade me welcome: yet my soul drew back,
      Guilty of dust and sin.
But quick-eyed Love, observing me grow slack
      From my first entrance in,
Drew nearer to me, sweetly questioning,
      If I lack'd anything.

A guest, I answer'd, worthy to be here:
      Love said, You shall be he.
I the unkind, ungrateful? Ah my dear,
      I cannot look on thee.
Love took my hand, and smiling did reply,
      Who made the eyes but I?

Truth Lord, but I have marr'd them: let my shame
      Go where it doth deserve.
And know you not, says Love, who bore the blame?
      My dear, then I will serve.
You must sit down, says Love, and taste my meat:
      So I did sit and eat.

George Herbert (1593-1633)

PART III
THE KINSMAN-REDEEMER

5. The levir and the goel

We must now stand apart from the text of Ruth for a while to examine two features of the laws and life of ancient Israel which are rather strange to us: the *levir* and the *goel*.

The first, the 'levir' (a Latin word translating the Hebrew for 'brother-in-law') concerns the family duties referred to in Ruth 3:13, which speaks of 'doing the part of the next of kin'. The levirate regulates marriage customs when the man of the house has died.

The second, the 'goel', is a near kinsman who acts as redeemer of persons or property. The verb *g'l* means to 'buy back' or 'redeem', but fundamentally its meaning is 'to protect'.[1]

These two family institutions are linked together at several points in the narrative of Ruth, and before looking in more detail at Ruth 3 and 4, we need to be clearer in our minds what these customs involve. We will take them in turn.

The levir

The levirate refers to an ancient marriage institution in which an in-law is involved. If a man dies without children, the 'name' of the dead man is perpetuated through the widow's marriage with another man (for example the man's brother), and through her having his children 'for' the dead man. Many gallons of scholarly ink have been expended on the purpose and practice of the levirate in the ancient Near East, and this is not the place to summarize all the discussion. Suffice it to say that a practice of this sort is attested in various forms in the Assyrian, Hittite and Ugaritic cultures,[2] as well as in ancient

---

[1] De Vaux, p. 21.   [2] *Ibid.*, p. 38.

Israel. There are in fact only three passages in the Old Testament in which the levirate practice is mentioned, and the apparent discrepancies between them have given rise to seemingly endless discussion.[3] One of these passages is the book of Ruth, and the other two, Genesis 38 and Deuteronomy 25:5–10, are both referred to in the book of Ruth.

We begin with the story of Judah and Tamar in Genesis 38. Judah has separated from his brothers (verse 1) and married a Canaanite woman. They have three sons, to the first of whom, Er, Judah gives a Canaanite woman in marriage. Her name was Tamar. Er dies without children (verse 7). So the family custom called the levirate becomes necessary. Judah tells the second son, Onan, to 'go in to your brother's wife, and perform the duty of a brother-in-law to her, and raise up offspring for your brother' (verse 8). The idea was that the child would be 'for' the dead older brother, Er. This would perpetuate Er's name, and also probably preserve his property.[4] A son born of this second union would be heir to the older brother. And the widow (also a 'capital asset' in the family) would be kept within the family, and not return to her father's house as an unmarried widow would do. Onan, however, is not keen to raise up children for his brother. He only pretends to do his brotherly duty, and for his lack of responsibility and lack of charity he incurs God's displeasure. He also dies (verse 10). According to the levirate custom, Judah is now duty bound to give his third son, Shelah, to Tamar. But he has seen what has happened to his first two sons, through their relationship with Tamar, and does not want to risk losing his only remaining son also (verse 11). So he tells Tamar that she will have to wait until Shelah is older. (From later in the story, it is clear that Judah never intended Shelah to become Tamar's levir at all: verse 26). Judah then tells Tamar to go temporarily back to 'her father's house'.

Tamar, however, realized that Judah wanted her out of his house permanently, and she now takes the initiative, through the guise of a harlot, to become pregnant by Judah himself. Clearly she believed that the levirate duty could be performed by the father-in-law as well as the brother-in-law. As a Canaanite worshipper of Ashtart, Tamar's action was understood in terms of a sacred cult prostitution of herself, rather than merely sordid harlotry. Such Canaanite customs were forbidden to the people of Yahweh.[5] Tamar, though, is the one who is praised by Judah (verse 26), and implicitly also by the narrator. Despite the guilt into which she and Judah are pushed by her action, it

---

[3] *Cf.* Leggett for a summary.

[4] *Cf.* G. von Rad, *Genesis* (SCM Press, [2]1963), p. 353.

[5] Dt. 23:17.

is the over-riding sense of duty to the dead brother's name which dominates the narrative. How important that the name of the dead man should not disappear without a heritage! How important that he should have a son!

When we move to Deuteronomy 25:5–10, the law seems in some ways to reflect a stricter understanding of the levirate practice than the narrative in Genesis 38 illustrates. The law reads thus:

> If brothers dwell together, and one of them dies and has no son, the wife of the dead shall not be married outside the family to a stranger; her husband's brother shall go in to her, and take her as his wife, and perform the duty of a husband's brother to her. And the first son whom she bears shall succeed to the name of his brother who is dead, that his name may not be blotted out of Israel.

Next, there is provision for the fact that the brother may not wish to perform this duty, and for the humiliating treatment he is to receive if he refuses:

> And if the man does not wish to take his brother's wife, then his brother's wife shall go up to the gate to the elders, and say, 'My husband's brother refuses to perpetuate his brother's name in Israel; he will not perform the duty of a husband's brother to me.' Then the elders of his city shall call him, and speak to him: and if he persists, saying, 'I do not wish to take her,' then his brother's wife shall go up to him in the presence of the elders, and pull his sandal off his foot, and spit in his face; and she shall answer and say, 'So shall it be done to the man who does not build up his brother's house.' And the name of his house shall be called in Israel, The house of him that had his sandal pulled off.

Some scholars believe[6] that this was an Israelite revision of an earlier Canaanite law. Whatever the final date of Deuteronomy, many are convinced that the law material contained in this section is from an early age[7] – and so reflects a very ancient custom. The law, as with some others in Deuteronomy, is in a casuistic style, rather like that of the early Book of the Covenant of Exodus 20:18–23. The special

[6] Cf. Leggett, p. 272.

[7] Cf. Eichrodt, p. 72. Cf. also W. F. Albright, *From the Stone Age to Christianity* (Johns Hopkins University Press, [2]1957), pp. 319f., in which the author says that 'the materials contained in the book were really believed to go back to Moses, and probably do reflect in general a true Mosaic atmosphere.'

points of interest here in Deuteronomy 25 are fourfold.

First, the law refers to 'brothers living together'. It assumes the arrangement of the 'extended family', and, as von Rad says,[8] gives the impression that the levirate law is considered valid only if this can be taken for granted. Perhaps Deuteronomy envisages a situation in which the head of the house is no longer alive – as was Judah in Genesis 38. Or perhaps it reflects a tightening up of the law as the custom developed.

Secondly, the Deuteronomic law emphasizes the sense of obligation on a brother to 'go in to' the 'wife of the dead' (verses 5, 7), and exercise the responsibility of a husband's brother to her. We are not concerned so much with the rights of the brother, as with the family obligation of continuing the dead man's name.

Thirdly, this passage from Deuteronomy shows that the obligation was not absolute (verses 7–9a). There was here, in contrast to the custom illustrated in Genesis 38, an element of choice.[9] There is a clear sense of shame in the brother's refusal, however, and the ceremony of verse 9 was intended to subject him to public humiliation.

Finally, the purpose of the levirate is given as a means of perpetuating the life and name of the deceased: 'that his name may not be blotted out of Israel', and 'to build up his house' (verses 6–9). Economic factors, such as keeping family property together, may well also have been significant; but it is the desire for children, especially male children, to keep the father's name and inheritance alive, which is so crucially important here. Leggett describes this as a 'duty of love',[10] and quotes Pedersen as saying:

If a man, after having contracted a marriage, dies without sons, then he dies entirely. It is this blotting out of life which is to be avoided. His nearest of kin, the brother, must perform this office of love in order to protect him from extermination. The wife, whose object in life is to bear him a son in whom his life is resurrected, must be enabled to do her duty towards him.[11]

Quite why the levirate custom grew up in Israel – or in the surrounding cultures – is not altogether clear. As Rowley remarks, 'the motives and ideas that gather round any custom are less simple

[8] G. von Rad, *Deuteronomy* (SCM Press, 1966), p. 155.

[9] Indeed, some argue that verses 7–9a show a late development of the law from the absolute perspective of verses 5–6, but that is not generally agreed.

[10] Leggett, p. 53.

[11] *Israel: Its Life and Culture* (1926), p. 78.

than our tidy minds desire. Customs arise out of a complex situation, for life is always complex, and they are retained for a complex of reasons.'[12]

What appears prominent in the Old Testament is the importance of the family name: that the childless deceased man should have a son, and that his widow was therefore entitled to motherhood as her expression of loyalty to her deceased husband, and her concern for the continuance of his inheritance.

The only other references to the levirate are in the book of Ruth,[13] particularly in chapters 3 and 4. Here we are given another illustration of the way the levirate custom was practised in Israel. The details here are not identical with the situation either of Genesis 38 or of Deuteronomy 25. There is no father-in-law involved for Ruth, nor is the situation that of 'brothers living together'. But there is no irreconcilable discrepancy between the accounts if we understand Deuteronomy 25 as setting out the legal form, and Genesis 38 and Ruth 4 as giving illustrations of the ways the custom operated in particular circumstances at particular times in Israel's history. Indeed, the whole institution seems to have been understood and interpreted more broadly in Ruth than the strict law of Deuteronomy 25 would indicate. If the levirate was, as Leggett suggested, especially a manifestation of family love, then it was quite proper for the requirements of family need to be predominant. Those, after all, are what this law was intended to safeguard.

The duties of the levirate in the story of Ruth devolve on the next of kin whoever he may be. This is why Naomi rejoices to find that Boaz is the man who helped Ruth – because 'he is one of our nearest kin'. He could quite properly be expected to act as levir for Ruth and make her the mother of a son for Elimelech. But we soon discover a twist in the story. As Boaz himself later makes clear, 'there is a kinsman nearer than I' (3:12). How, in the providence of God (as Naomi would say), this nearest of kin is unable in fact to fulfil the duties of levir, so that the joyous task reverts to Boaz, we must leave until we have looked at that other ancient institution intertwined with the levirate in the story of Ruth: the goel.

[12] Rowley, p. 177.

[13] Some have argued that the laws of Lv. 18:16 and 20:21, forbidding the marriage of a brother and sister-in-law, are a final stage of development in which the levirate custom was abolished by law. But not all commentators are sure that Lv. 18:16 is abrogating the levirate; rather it could be legislating against illegal sexual relations between a brother and sister-in-law, and does not refer to a marriage after the death of the brother. It is quite

The goel[14]

We have noted in earlier discussion of the story of Ruth that there was a strong sense of family solidarity among the people of Yahweh. The members of the family had a duty to care for and protect each other. There were certain situations defined by law in the institution of the goel in ancient Israel, in which these obligations had to be expressed in action. Although, as de Vaux tells us, there are analogies among other peoples,[15] the goel institution in Israel took a special form – special because, as we shall see, it was related to Israel's special status as the covenant people of Yahweh.

We mentioned that the goel is the 'protector' – a near kinsman whose duty it is in certain circumstances to act as 'redeemer' in situations of family need. Four such situations are described in the Pentateuch.

In Leviticus 25:25–28, after a reminder that the land belongs to Yahweh, we find this possibility envisaged:

> If your brother becomes poor, and sells part of his property, then his next of kin shall come and redeem what his brother has sold. If a man has no one to redeem it, and then himself becomes prosperous and finds sufficient means to redeem it, let him reckon the years since he sold it and pay back the overpayment to the man to whom he sold it; and he shall return to his property. But if he has not sufficient means to get it back for himself, then what he sold shall remain in the hand of him who bought it until the year of jubilee; in the jubilee it shall be released, and he shall return to his property.

This stresses the importance to a man of maintaining his own property and inheritance (until the year of Jubilee), and of the role of the 'next of kin' – the goel – to redeem property which has been sold. The goel is the responsible next of kin who acts to prevent property being lost to the family. It is this redemption of property which underlies some of the narrative of Ruth 4.

---

possible to understand Lv. 18:16 as referring to adultery. Lv. 20:21, by contrast, may be forbidding a marriage with a deceased brother's wife when she has already borne a son to the deceased brother during his lifetime. This would explain the mildness of the penalty for infringement (childlessness), whereas if the brother was alive, the offence would be adultery, and the penalty could be death. *Cf.* Leggett, p. 281.

[14] *Cf.* Leggett, p. 292; *cf.* also de Vaux, p. 21.

[15] De Vaux, *ibid.*

Secondly, in Leviticus 25:47–49, the redemption is not of property, but of a person:

> If a stranger or sojourner with you becomes rich, and your brother beside him becomes poor and sells himself to the stranger or sojourner with you, or to a member of the stranger's family, then after he is sold he may be redeemed; one of his brothers may redeem him, or his uncle, or his cousin may redeem him, or a near kinsman belonging to his family may redeem him; or if he grows rich he may redeem himself.

The goel here, the kinsman-redeemer, acts to set free a member of his family who because of financial hardship had been forced to sell himself as a slave.

The third circumstance is mentioned in Numbers 35:16ff., which discusses one of the most serious aspects of family solidarity: that of blood vengeance. The blood of a murdered kinsman must be avenged by the death of him who shed it, or by the death of one of his family. On this de Vaux comments:

> In contrast with Bedouin law . . . Israelite legislation does not allow compensation in money, alleging for this a religious motive: blood which is shed defiles the land in which Yahweh dwells, and must be expiated by the blood of him who shed it.[16]

The law concerned reads: 'The avenger of blood shall himself put the murderer to death; when he meets him, he shall put him to death' (verse 19). Being the 'avenger of blood' was one of the most solemn responsibilities of the goel in the desert community.[17] It underlined in a most marked way the family group's collective responsibility to care for the weak and oppressed members.

Finally, the goel could act as trustee in such payments as were due in order to make restitution for a wrong caused by the sin of a kinsman. Numbers 5:8 refers to such a role for the goel: 'If the man has no kinsman to whom restitution may be made for the wrong, the restitution for wrong shall go to the Lord for the priest.' Again the goel is an institution of family solidarity and a reminder of collective responsibility.

As Leggett points out, these duties among the people of Israel flow from the covenant relationship into which they had been called by Yahweh. Leggett says:

---

[16] *Ibid.*, p. 12.　　[17] *Cf.* also Jos. 20:3, 5, 9; 2 Sa. 14:11.

These duties, which were all prescribed in the Old Testament laws, are only understandable from the background of the covenant in which Israel as a people became Yahweh's own unique possession (Ex. 19:5) among whom he dwelt (Ex. 25:8). The land was Yahweh's and was given to Israel through his saving intervention as the powerful Lord of history. Therefore the land was not to be sold in perpetuity (Lv. 25:23) but was rather to be redeemed (Lv. 25:24). Yahweh had redeemed the people of Israel out of Egypt, by which act they became his servants (Lv. 25:37, 55). Accordingly, an impoverished Israelite who has sold himself into slavery was to be redeemed by the goel (Lv. 25:55). It is evident, then, that the responsibilities and privileges of the goel institution are derived from Yahweh's redemptive action in delivering Israel out of Egyptian bondage and by bringing her into the Promised Land... The relationship of Israelites to each other in terms of the goel institution is grounded in their common covenant relationship with Yahweh: 'And I will walk among you, and will be your God, and you shall be my people' (Lv. 26:12).[18]

The goel institution thus illustrates the emphasis in the Old Testament on the people of God as a community, and on the solidarity of the kinship group. The responsibilities of the goel to act as redeemer are *kinship* responsibilities. But they are also a reflection of a bond stronger than physical relationship: that of *covenant loyalty*. The special emphasis on the goel institution in Israel, therefore, must be seen in the special covenant relationship between the people and Yahweh, and the way in which the whole of life was related to him through the covenant.

Land and people

One of the interesting features of the 'goel' function within the covenant is that the goel can redeem both land and people. While in the pentateuchal laws personal values always take precedence over material concerns, the land – the material world – is never unimportant. And this matters in the biblical understanding of human life. It is a constant feature of both Old Testament and New that, despite the differences of emphasis on 'body' and on 'soul', the most important thing to say about human beings is that our lives are a unity: a psychosomatic unity with spiritual potential. In the Old Testament, concepts such as heart, soul, flesh and spirit, and words for various

[18] Leggett, pp. 292f.

parts of the body (mouth, hand, feet), are often interchangeable in Hebrew poetry. Each can stand for the 'whole' man, expressed in different ways. There is no body/soul dualism.

Nor in the New Testament is there any thought of the soul as separated from the body – rather the physical body is the vehicle of the experience with this physical world of our whole selves – as the 'spiritual' body will be in the resurrection. We need to beware of thinking that there is only part of life which is relevant to God: only part of life which can be redeemed. No: our whole selves, psychological and physical, are the concern of the redeemer, and our personal being within the wider context of the whole natural order. Paul in Romans 8:18ff. indicates that the whole physical world is 'groaning' with the birthpangs of a new creation – the redeemer of the world redeems not only me, and not only people, but the whole natural world order also. Such a unified view will help us to avoid the disastrous duality of much modern thinking which tends to keep God 'safe' by restricting him only to a corner of our concerns. Within the covenant purposes of God, the kinsman-redeemer has responsibilities to the material as well as the personal realms.

Yahweh, the Goel

The word 'goel', or verbs and associated nouns from the same word root, which are used of the Israelite kinsman-redeemer, are used by the people of Israel also of their covenant God, Yahweh. In the early days when God made himself known to Moses as Yahweh, and commissioned him to negotiate with Pharaoh for the release of the Israelite slaves from Egypt, he told Moses:

> Say therefore to the people of Israel, 'I am the Lord, and I will bring you out from under the burdens of the Egyptians, and I will deliver you from their bondage, and I will *redeem* (g'1) you with an outstretched arm and with great acts of judgment, and I will take you for my people, and I will be your God; and you shall know that I am the Lord your God, who has brought you out from under the burdens of the Egyptians. And I will bring you into the land which I swore to give to Abraham, to Isaac, and to Jacob; I will give it to you for a possession. I am the Lord.'[19]

The central focus of the calling of the people to be God's covenant people, and his promise of a new hope in a new land, is the act of

[19] Ex. 6:6–8.

94

redemption from Egypt. How important that the Lord is their kinsman, their redeemer!

Later, we read, especially in Isaiah 40 – 55, God is again and again described as 'the Lord your Redeemer, the Holy One of Israel'.[20] Likewise, Jeremiah speaks of God's reference to the oppression of the peoples of Israel and Judah under captivity, and then his word 'Their Redeemer is strong; the Lord of hosts is his name. He will surely plead their cause.'[21] This, too, is how the psalmists understood their God: 'my rock and my redeemer'.[22] 'Draw near to me, redeem me, set me free because of my enemies!'[23] 'He delivers the needy when he calls, the poor and him who has no helper. He has pity on the weak and needy, and saves the lives of the needy. From oppression and violence he redeems (g'1) their life; and precious is their blood in his sight.'[24] 'Thou art the God who workest wonders...thou didst with thy arm redeem thy people.'[25] The Lord 'redeems your life from the Pit, who crowns you with steadfast love and mercy.'[26] He 'delivered' the people from the power of the enemy.[27] 'Let the redeemed of the Lord say so, whom he has redeemed from trouble.'[28]

God is thus understood as the sort of God who stands by the oppressed, who calls a people to be his own covenant family by rescuing them from slavery, who with his mighty arm liberates the captives and offers them a new freedom and a new hope. This is an expression of his love and mercy; a deep concern for the material, emotional and spiritual welfare of his people. This is the character which is to be seen also in the kinsman-redeemer of Israel – the one who by his actions on behalf of those in need is demonstrating within family relationships something of the character of their covenant God. And from their position of helpless need, it is for this sort of expression of love that Naomi and Ruth look when Naomi breaks the good news to her daughter-in-law about their family link with Boaz.

Redemption costs

The primary emphasis in the word 'goel' is thus the general one of family obligation. Within this, particularly in the use of 'goel' with reference to human needs, the word also carries the sense of the payment of price.[29] This implies the idea of effort and cost on the part

---

[20] Is. 41:14; *cf*. 43:14; 44:6, 24; 47:4; 48:17; 49:26; 54:5, 8; 59:20; 60:16; 63:16.
[21] Je. 50:34.   [22] Ps. 19:14; *cf*. 78:35.
[23] Ps. 69:18.   [24] Ps. 72:12ff.   [25] Ps. 77:14f.
[26] Ps. 103:4.   [27] Ps. 106:10.   [28] Ps. 107:2.
[29] *Cf*. L. Morris, *The Apostolic Preaching of the Cross* (Inter-Varsity Press, ³1965), p. 20.

of the redeemer for the sake of the kinsman. Sometimes it means the payment of a ransom, a redemption price, as a result of the kinship relationship. In the passages in which the Lord is referred to as goel, there is often implied something of the costliness of redemption. In Isaiah 52:10, after describing the joyful return of the exiles, the prophet exclaims: 'The Lord has bared his holy arm before the eyes of all the nations.' As Michael Green comments on this: 'the redemption of God's people was costly'.[30] Likewise in Isaiah 43:3–4, the idea of costly purchase in redemption is very evident: 'I am the Lord your God, the Holy One of Israel, your Saviour. I give Egypt as your ransom, Ethiopia and Seba in exchange for you. Because you are precious in my eyes, and honoured, and I love you, I give men in return for you, peoples in exchange for your life.' Green quotes Westcott's comment: 'It cannot be said that God paid to the Egyptian oppressor any price for the redemption of his people. On the other hand the idea of the exertion of a mighty force, the idea that the "redemption" costs much, is everywhere present. The force may be represented by divine might, or love, or self-sacrifice, which become finally identical.'[31]

Sometimes, as Leon Morris notes,[32] the Bible uses redemption terminology of the saving actions of Yahweh precisely to make this stress on his 'effort'. 'I will redeem you with an outstretched arm';[33] 'Thou art the God who workest wonders, who hast manifested thy might among the peoples. Thou didst with thy arm redeem thy people.'[34] The effort, says Morris, is regarded as the 'price' which gives point to the redemption metaphor. Yahweh's action is at cost *to himself*.

As we shall later emphasize in the redeeming action of Boaz,[35] to act as a goel in his circumstances would have been very costly. It involved personal sacrifice. It is important that we hold together these two aspects of the functions of goel – the relational aspects of redeemership, and price-paying as the meaning of redemption.

A future and a hope

We have earlier suggested that one of the purposes of the book of Ruth is to expound the meaning of 'redemption'. It is not insignificant that

[30] E. M. B. Green, *The Meaning of Salvation* (Hodder and Stoughton, 1965), p. 30.
[31] Green, *ibid.*, quoting B. F. Westcott, *Hebrews* (1892), p. 296.
[32] Morris, *Apostolic Preaching*, p. 22.
[33] Ex. 6:6.   [34] Ps. 77:14–15.
[35] See below, section 7.

Paul in particular in the New Testament focuses much of his thinking
on the person of Jesus Christ the redeemer in the way the author of
Ruth does on Boaz. As D. A. Leggett comments:

> In the actions of Boaz as goel we see foreshadowed the saving work of
> Jesus Christ, his later descendant. As Boaz had the right of redemp-
> tion and yet clearly was under no obligation to intervene on Ruth's
> behalf, so it was with Christ. As Boaz, seeing the plight of the poor
> widows, came to their rescue because his life was governed by
> Yahweh and his laws, so also of the Messiah it is prophesied that his
> life would be governed by the law of God and that he would deal
> justly and equitably with the poor and with those who were
> oppressed (Ps. 72:2, 4, 12, 13; Is. 11:4).[36]

Paul uses the 'kinship model' of the atonement in Christ in his
writing in Romans 5 – 8.[37] Christ is associated closely with us (as Boaz
with Ruth), being born 'in the likeness of sinful flesh' (8:3). He pays
the price of redemption demanded by our old master – his own death.
'There could be no other price if he was fully to associate himself with
us in our position under the sway of sin and death.' But such a Goel
could not be held by the power of death. He rose from death, 'bringing
with him those with whom he had associated himself.' We were
'buried with him... united with him... crucified with him' (6:4–6)
and so we will also be 'alive to God in Christ Jesus' (6:11). God's object
in all this is expressed in 8:29: 'Those whom he foreknew he also
predestined to be conformed to the image of his Son, in order that he
might be the first-born among many brethren.' A new family has been
created by the intervention of our great Kinsman-Redeemer. We are
adopted into God's family (8:15) and so are children of God – and
fellow heirs with Christ (8:16–17). And with us, the whole created
order will be 'set free from its bondage to decay, and obtain the
glorious liberty of the children of God' (8:18ff.).

Christ our Goel, like Boaz for Ruth, is related to us, able and
willing to redeem. As we think further on the way the author of Ruth
sought to expound the meaning of redemption, and to focus his
readers' minds on the figure of the kinsman-redeemer, we, from this
side of the cross, can rejoice in God's provision in Christ for our
redemption into a new family of his children within a new creation.

[36] Leggett, p. 298.
[37] Cf. S. Motyer's exposition, 'Always being given up to death', Churchman, 95.4
(1981), pp. 299ff., on which this paragraph draws heavily.

We now belong! We have been welcomed home! We have been given a future and a hope.

We now turn back to the book of Ruth and remind ourselves that the crucial turning-point in Naomi's feelings from despair to hope came in 2:20 at the end of that eventful day in which Ruth happened to glean in Boaz' field. 'Blessed be he by the Lord', cries Naomi in delight on hearing that Boaz was the generous farmer who had taken Ruth under his care. 'The man is a relative of ours, one of our redeemers — our goel!' From this point we can understand that for Naomi and for Ruth the existence of a goel holds out the promise of protection, of help, of redemption. If there is a goel, a near kinsman pledged to family solidarity, perhaps — in the absence of others — he can be persuaded to become a levir. In him lies their future and their hope. Perhaps Boaz the goel will be the one by whom the family name of Elimelech can be preserved through the child of a levirate marriage. How can Naomi bring this desired conclusion about, to the benefit not only of the name of Elimelech, but also of her beloved daughter-in-law Ruth, who had come to take refuge under the wings of her covenant God?

3:1–18

6. Faith active in love

Naomi's initiative (3:1–5)

Then Naomi her mother-in-law said to her, 'My daughter, should I not seek a home for you, that it may be well with you? ²Now is not Boaz our kinsman, with whose maidens you were? See, he is winnowing barley tonight at the threshing floor. ³Wash therefore and anoint yourself, and put on your best clothes and go down to the threshing floor; but do not make yourself known to the man until he has finished eating and drinking. ⁴But when he lies down, observe the place where he lies; then, go and uncover his feet and lie down; and he will tell you what to do.' ⁵And she replied, 'All that you say I will do.'

The initiative in the narrative now stays very firmly with Naomi. Her concern is for Ruth's welfare. Moffatt translates her words to Ruth, 'I must see you settled in life.' She therefore naturally wanted Ruth to marry again. She had expressed this before back in Moab (1:11), but there the prospects of marriage had been extremely remote. Now the news that Boaz met Ruth has changed the despair into a new hope. For Boaz is a close relative. Did Naomi think that he was their nearest of kin – their goel? Did she know that in fact there was another near kinsman (3:12)? If so, was she by this approach to Boaz trying to force the other to declare his colours? If she knew of this other man, the approach which she was now urging Ruth to make towards Boaz underlines the fact that our author gradually makes clearer from now on, that any action from Boaz could not possibly rest on the requirements of law, but only on Boaz' willingness and generosity. What is clear is that Naomi saw the way forward in planning for Ruth to ask Boaz to act for her as levir. He was a near kinsman: let them ask him to help and protect them. Would he be willing to 'do the part of the next

of kin' by entering a levirate marriage with Ruth, and so fathering a
son for Ruth's (and so for Naomi's) dead husband? The time had come
for careful preparations to that end, and Naomi takes steps to discover
how a meeting between Boaz and Ruth can be staged. Tonight Boaz is
on duty at the threshing floor; this is the moment for action.

It was the responsibility of parents in those days to make arrange-
ments for marriage. We can see this illustrated, for example, in the
way young Samson 'saw one of the daughters of the Philistines', and
came back to his father and mother asking them to 'get her for me as
my wife'.[1] Naomi here takes on parental responsibilities for Ruth.
Boaz is *our kinsman*: related to Naomi through Elimelech and to Ruth
through Elimelech's son Mahlon. That evening Boaz will be winnowing
barley at the *threshing floor*. From late afternoon until near sunset a
wind rises from the sea. Boaz will be at the threshing floor on the
hillside outside the village at that time, throwing the grain, trodden
out by the animals, against the wind for the husks to blow away.

Ruth is to *wash* and *anoint* herself, and then put on a heavy mantle as
a covering, and no doubt to prevent herself from being recognized. She
is to prepare herself 'as a bride prepares for her marriage'.[2] A similar
description is found in the writing of Ezekiel,[3] in which the Lord
speaks in terms of his love to Jerusalem, 'plights his troth' to her, and
then (he says) 'bathed you with water and washed off your blood from
you, and anointed you with oil. I clothed you also with embroidered
cloth and shod you with leather...'

Naomi is preparing Ruth to make clear to Boaz that she wants him
to marry her. Then Ruth is to go down to the threshing floor and wait
until Boaz has finished his meal. She is to make a careful note of the
place where he lies down to sleep, so that later on she can go and lie
near to him. All the preparations for this night-time visit, the place,
the way of approach, the timing, all are geared to making it clear that
Ruth is asking Boaz for (levirate) marriage.

Ruth's courageous loyalty (3:6–9)

*So she went down to the threshing floor and did just as her mother-in-law had
told her. [7]And when Boaz had eaten and drunk, and his heart was merry, he
went to lie down at the end of the heap of grain. Then she came softly, and
uncovered his feet, and lay down. [8]At midnight the man was startled, and
turned over, and behold, a woman lay at his feet! [9]He said, 'Who are you?'*

---

[1] Jdg. 14:2.   [2] Cooke.   [3] Ezk. 16:9ff.

And she answered, 'I am Ruth, your maidservant; spread your skirt over your maidservant, for you are next of kin.'

Obediently, Ruth did just as her mother-in-law had told her. It is not spelled out here what motivated Ruth beyond this committed loyalty to Naomi. As Boaz later remarked, there may well have been much more attractive younger men available to Ruth (3:10) than this older bachelor, had she chosen to 'go after' them. But Ruth has come to learn how important a husband's inheritance and a male heir were to the people of Yahweh in those times: how important the inheritance of Elimelech and Mahlon were to Naomi. Naomi, Ruth knows, is too old to bear children (1:11). Orpah had gone back to Moab. The important duty now falls to her. Quite apart, therefore, from any personal wish for a husband and family, which we can well imagine Ruth felt, she knows that she is now part of the covenant family of Yahweh, and she is willing to take her part in the levirate custom for Yahweh's sake and for that of the inheritance of one of his people. And that moment has now come.

Harvest time was also feasting time,[4] and after the party, Boaz lay down to sleep, observed by the as yet unrecognized Ruth. When he was asleep, she crept up to him and *lay down* at his *feet* – a place of humility; a place even of supplication. Some time passed. Then in the author's vivid way he tells us the time: *midnight*! Boaz was *startled*. He sat up. *Behold, a woman lay at his feet!*

We can imagine the tense whisper, '*Who are you*? What do you want?' And then Ruth makes herself known with characteristic humility: '*I am Ruth, your maidservant.*' But why was she there? She asks her crucial question: 'Will you *spread your skirt over your maidservant, for you are* my goel?' This was a delicate request for marriage. The 'spreading of the skirt' is referred to in the passage from Ezekiel to which we referred, in the Lord's word of love to Jerusalem:

When I passed by you again and looked upon you, behold, you were at the age for love; and I spread my skirt over you, and covered your nakedness; yea, I plighted my troth to you and entered into a covenant with you, says the Lord God, and you became mine.[5]

Cooke quotes an interesting illustration of this practice by which a kinsman claimed a widow as wife:

---

[4] *Cf.* Is. 9:3.   [5] Ezk. 16:8.

The custom prevailed among the early Arabs; a good illustration is given in Tabari's commentary on the Koran... 'In the Jahiliya, when a man's father or brother or son died and left a widow, the dead man's heir, if he came at once and threw his garment over her, had the right to marry her under the dowry of (i.e. already paid by) her (deceased) lord, or to give her in marriage and take her dowry.'[6]

Boaz certainly understood Ruth's request in terms of a desire for marriage, as we can gather from his response. 'You have made this last kindness greater than the first, in that you have not gone after young men' (3:10). Against the thought that Ruth was doing something improper, or even immoral, in asking for levirate marriage in this way – a procedure which would have been quite out of place in an ordinary marriage – the author makes clear that she feels confident to do so because Boaz is *next of kin*. In fact, as we discover soon in the story, there was a kinsman nearer than he, but the point remains: Ruth is asking Boaz as goel to act as her levir. It was clearly a risky undertaking. Ruth is placing herself in a situation of extreme vulnerability, in which she could easily be taken advantage of. 'That she involves herself in such a painful situation is the heroism of faithfulness. She desires nothing for herself, only an heir for her husband.'[7] The phrase 'spread your skirt', which Keil and Delitzsch translate as 'the corner of the counterpane',[8] reminds us (though it is not an identical expression) of the 'wings' of Yahweh under which Ruth had come to take refuge (2:12). It is because she now belongs within the covenant people of Yahweh that she is seeking the protection of the 'wings' of Boaz in marriage.

Boaz' gracious generosity (3:10–18)

And he said, 'May you be blessed by the Lord, my daughter; you have made this last kindness greater than the first, in that you have not gone after young men, whether poor or rich. [11]*And now, my daughter, do not fear, I will do for you all that you ask, for all my fellow townsmen know that you are a woman of worth.* [12]*And now it is true that I am a near kinsman, yet there is a kinsman nearer than I.* [13]*Remain this night, and in the morning, if he will do the part of the next of kin for you, well; let him do it; but if he is not willing to do the part of the next of kin for you, then, as the Lord lives, I will do the part of the next of kin for you. Lie down until the morning.'*

[14]*So she lay at his feet until the morning, but arose before one could recognize*

---

[6] Cooke, p. 11.   [7] Gunkel, quoted in Leggett, p. 194.
[8] Keil and Delitzsch, p. 484.

another; and he said, 'Let it not be known that the woman came to the threshing floor.' [15]*And he said, 'Bring the mantle you are wearing and hold it out.' So she held it, and he measured out six measures of barley, and laid it upon her; then she went into the city.* [16]*And when she came to her mother-in-law, she said, 'How did you fare, my daughter?' Then she told her all that the man had done for her,* [17]*saying, 'These six measures of barley he gave to me, for he said, "You must not go back empty-handed to your mother-in-law."' She replied, 'Wait, my daughter, until you learn how the matter turns out, for the man will not rest, but will settle the matter today.'*

We have commented earlier on the meaning of *ḥesed*, the word used in 1:8 and 2:20 of God, and used here of Ruth (*this last kindness*). Ruth's steadfastness and faithfulness are seen in her willingness not to put her own likely preference for the *young men* before her commitment to her new family obligations. This calls forth from Boaz a prayer for God's blessing on her. Ruth is now a member of God's covenant family, and is showing her 'faith active in love'.[9] And it is not as though she had no choice! Clearly she would have been attractive to others. All the towns-folk who gather at the city gate for conversation or for business have been talking about her, have spoken of her virtue — calling her a *woman of worth*, even (as Knox rather freely translates) a 'bride worth winning'. The word *worth* is that used also of richness and wealth, of strength and valour, of virtue and character. It described Boaz, the man of influence (2:1). It describes the 'virtuous woman' (AV) or 'good wife' (RSV) of Proverbs 31:10. It points to Ruth's strength of character.

In response to Ruth's questions, Boaz promises his help — in fact, he will act immediately the night is over. Ruth is not to fear: *I will do for you all that you ask*. Cooke points to the subtle change from Naomi's word to Ruth in 3:4 (*he will tell you what to do*), to the way Ruth herself suggested what Boaz was to tell (*all that you ask*, 3:11). 'The coincidence', says Cooke, 'was guided by Jehovah's good providence.' In the preparation of hearts and minds and attitudes which led to this response from Boaz, rather than any other response he was quite free to make, Cooke rightly sees the over-ruling providential grace of God.

As we have said, Boaz clearly understands Ruth's action and question as a request for levirate marriage. There have been commentators who believe that Boaz is concerned only about redeeming property, and would have understood Ruth's reference to the goel in those terms. Certainly the question of property redemption occurs in Ruth 4, but it is inconceivable in the light of his reference to the 'young men', and to

[9] *Cf.* Gal. 5:6 NEB.

103

the levirate institution in 3:13, that he has misunderstood Ruth's meaning. In any case, if the question of Naomi's land-redemption was the issue, she should have gone herself to negotiate, and not sent Ruth to wake Boaz in the middle of the night. No, Boaz knew perfectly well what Ruth was asking. He did not regard it as immoral or impertinent. He recognized that she was honouring a family obligation, and regarded himself as honoured to have been asked.

It appears from Deuteronomy 25 and Genesis 38 that the initiative for redeeming action would come from the goel himself. Only if he was unwilling to act would the widow make a move. Why, then, has not Boaz taken the initiative in this case? The answer must lie in the existence of another kinsman, *a kinsman nearer than I*. If anyone should have acted, this other man – had he known the situation – was the one. Genesis 38 also indicates that there is an order of preference in the exercise of the levirate. The obligation for levirate marriage falls on to this 'other kinsman' before it falls on Boaz. Only *if he is not willing to do the part of the next of kin* can Boaz act as levir.

Boaz, therefore, is under no legal obligation to act at all, within the terms of the levirate marriage. Further, the pentateuchal laws concerning the goel, as we have seen, would not have required any action from Boaz. There was a broad understanding of the function of the goel in the Old Testament, however, which did not restrict his duties simply to fulfilling the legal code. It was rather a covenantal and moral obligation to act on behalf of a kinsman in need, whatever that need may be. We have seen how the word 'goel' was applied to Yahweh in his very broad expression of compassion for the oppressed, and his activity in redeeming the captives, and helping the needy. Leggett quotes Schoneveld as saying:

> It is expected from a redeemer that he will not only meet the written obligations, but also that, under such circumstances, he will show his *ḥeseḏ* [faithful covenant love], that is his preparedness to help on the basis of an existing relationship. The greater his resources, the more the redeemer *could* do; the more *ḥeseḏ* he had, the more he *wanted* to do.[10]

In this situation of an advance by the two widows, we are to assume that this was the view of the goel which they shared. They could expect nothing from Boaz as of right. But they believed they could trust themselves to his loving mercy and compassionate generosity. And they were rewarded.

Boaz expressed his care for Ruth not only in his positive response to her question, but in other ways too. She is not to go home on her own in the middle of the night – a course of considerable danger, we may well assume – but is to enjoy the protection of staying with him. And when she does go in the dim light of dawn, she is to be careful to keep her visit a secret. Boaz is concerned that there will be no misunderstandings by others of this night-time visit, which could jeopardize the course on which they are both now set. Leon Morris[11] quotes the Mishnah in which it is noted that a man suspected of having sexual relations with a Gentile woman was excluded from performing levirate marriage with her. Maybe such a taboo was known to Boaz: he wants to give no impression that anything improper has happened. Certainly, as Boaz was aware of a 'nearer kinsman', he would not have wanted him at this stage to know anything of Boaz' feelings for Ruth. As Rowley suggests:

> If the nearer kinsman had had any idea that Boaz wanted to marry Ruth, he might have been ready to exploit the situation. And Boaz knew enough of human nature to guess what this might have meant. The kinsman might have needed inducing to renounce his claim, or even to withhold a charge of adultery against Ruth for what had already happened, so that his children's patrimony might have been not alone unimpaired, but substantially improved! Also Ruth was in real danger, and it needed all the resources of Boaz to cope with the situation. He kept his own desire for Ruth completely in the background, and appeared primarily as the economic benefactor of Naomi.[12]

Furthermore, a large gift of *six measures of barley*, apparently for Ruth to share with Naomi, confirms Boaz' goodwill to both the women.[13] It is interesting that Ruth reports Boaz as saying that she *must not go back* to Naomi *empty-handed*. Did Ruth cunningly elaborate this to ingratiate Boaz with his prospective mother-in-law? We do not know. But the last time we met this reference to emptiness was in Naomi's despair of 1:21 – 'I went away full, and the Lord has brought me back empty.' As Morris comments on 3:17, 'her "empty" days are over!'

[11] Morris, p. 293, quoting *Yeb.* 2.8.   [12] Rowley, p. 190.

[13] There is some doubt as to which 'measure' is meant. Six 'ephahs' would be an impossibly large amount – six times what Ruth had gleaned in a day (2:17). Six 'omers' (one tenth of an ephah) would be less than a day's gleaning – yet the way Boaz has to 'lay' the load on Ruth makes it look like a large amount. Some commentators suggest six 'seahs' which is about 2 ephahs = 88 pounds; a very heavy but not impossible load; a very generous gift.

Naomi greets Ruth on her return to the city: *How did you fare?* The AV reads 'Who are you?' This may, like the blind Isaac's question to his son Jacob[14] when he was unsure of his identity, mean that Ruth was hard to recognize – particularly with this unexpected load on her head – in the dim morning light. But more likely, as the form of Ruth's answer would indicate, this is a Hebrew way of asking how she had got on. Naomi sees the barley as a token of the man's goodwill, and takes him at his word that he *will not rest* until *the matter* is settled. The complication of the nearer kinsman may not have entered into Naomi's earlier thoughts. How Boaz handles this in such a way that Naomi's hopes are richly fulfilled, we discover in the final chapter of Ruth.

The grace of the redeemer

We can now begin to see more clearly how our author understands the grace and providence of God. We have earlier noticed his understanding of grace through God's providential over-ruling of events, how there is a second story being written by and through the events of human choices and human circumstances. We noticed how there is often a special grace through the circumstances of suffering, which introduces us, in a way not available through other means, to the resources of God's almighty comfort. We then saw how grace was linked with provision in a very material way through the gleaning opportunities open to Ruth, and through Boaz' further generosity. And now we are introduced to the redeemer. The benefits of God's gracious providence in the mind of the author of Ruth are linked with the person of Boaz, the kinsman-redeemer, through whom these benefits in large measure come.

From our New Testament perspective we can also see how much of God's gracious providence to us is linked in the mind of the New Testament writers to the person of Christ. It is in him that God has set forth his purposes for the world 'as a plan for the fullness of time, to unite all things in him, things in heaven and things on earth'.[15] This is the 'eternal purpose which he has realized in Christ Jesus our Lord, in whom we have boldness and confidence of access through our faith in him'.[16] It is in Christ that we come to understand God as 'the Father of mercies and God of all comfort, who comforts us in all our affliction'.[17] 'For as we share abundantly in Christ's sufferings, so through Christ we share abundantly in comfort too.'[18] Furthermore, it is through Christ that the rich resources of God's provision are made over to us. We know Christ, says Calvin, as we know his benefits. And we 'know

[14] Gn. 27:18.   [15] Eph. 1:10.   [16] Eph. 3:11f.
[17] 2 Cor. 1:3–4.   [18] 2 Cor. 1:5.

the grace of our Lord Jesus Christ, that though he was rich, yet for your sake he became poor, so that by his poverty you might become rich.'[19] And through him, whether our circumstances are of 'abasement' or 'abundance',[20] we can learn in whatever state we are, to be content, in the confidence that 'my God will supply every need . . . according to his riches in glory in Christ Jesus'.[21]

Christ, our Kinsman-Redeemer, brings with him 'the forgiveness of our sins, and all other benefits of his passion', calling us to be members of his family, entering with us into the pains of our suffering and bearing them with us, encouraging us to trust our Father in heaven to give us day by day our daily bread, and welcoming us ultimately to the wedding banquet of the Lamb when – as the consummation of our future and our hope – we, with the great multitude which no man can number, will join in the song of 'Hallelujah! For the Lord our God the Almighty reigns!'[22]

Law and love

There is a tendency among some Christians to polarize law and love. Sometimes law is thought to be characteristic of the Old Testament, and love the radical new proclamation of the New. No such polarity between the Testaments exists in the minds of the biblical authors. Indeed it is on the Old Testament texts of 'love to God' and 'love to neighbour'[23] that Jesus hangs all the law and the prophets.[24] There is no polarity between law and love themselves in the biblical writings, either. And certainly not in the book of Ruth. Boaz is a law-abiding person. For him the law gives guidance for living as a person within the covenant family of God. But for him, law is not a legal code only, it is a reminder that he is part of the family of the covenant of God. Law for Boaz is torah (fatherly instruction from God), not a moralistic legal code. God's torah is guidance in loving. It is the application of the character of the covenant God to the specific situations of daily life.

When Jesus tells his hearers that he does not come to abolish the law, but to fulfil it,[25] he surely is also understanding 'torah' not in terms of a legalistic code, but as the fatherly instruction of the covenant God to his children. And Jesus makes explicit what is implicit in the narrative of Boaz, that love, though never less than law, always goes beyond it for the sake of the other. Jesus penetrates to the heart of the purpose of law, behind the scribal interpretations which had reduced it to an all-sufficient code, to indicate the sort of right-

---

[19] 2 Cor. 8:9.   [20] Phil. 4:12.   [21] Phil. 4:19.   [22] Rev. 19:6.
[23] Dt. 6:4f.; Lv. 19:18.   [24] Mt. 22:37f.   [25] Mt. 5:17.

eousness (right relationship) which exceeds that of the scribes and Pharisees of his time.[26] The law is guidance in loving, and gives particular illustrations of the meaning of loving obedience in certain situations.[27] To concentrate on 'love' alone soon robs the word of any content. It can be used as the cover for any and all behaviour which 'seems good' or 'feels right'. There is no guard against sinful self-indulgence, or plain stupidity. To concentrate on 'law' alone, outside the covenant context of redemption and glad response to grace, soon transforms law into legalism, morality into moralism, and the liberty of faith into the struggle to keep the rules – a bondage from which Christ has set us free.

Let us labour to articulate an ethic of 'allegiance'[28] to our redeeming Lord, who – as a gift of his grace – has given us a law to guide us in loving. And not only so, he has written the law within our hearts by the Holy Spirit he has given to us. We need the Word, to deliver us from falling into a morality of subjectivism and relativity. We need the Spirit to implant the rich and other-regarding motivation which floods the law with the meaning of love, and which enables us to go beyond its strict letter, in the direction in which it points, for the sake of the other, and out of glad response to Christ's redeeming love.

Boaz gives us further illustration of the meaning of love going beyond law in his handling of the complex negotiations to which we now turn in Ruth 4.

[26] Mt. 5:20.   [27] Mt. 5:21–48.
[28] *Cf.* Helen Oppenheimer, *The Character of Christian Morality* (Faith Press, ²1974), pp. 53f.

Jesu, Lover of my soul,
    Let me to thy bosom fly,
While the nearer waters roll,
    While the tempest still is high;
Hide me, O my Saviour, hide,
    Till the storm of life is past;
Safe into the haven guide;
    O receive my soul at last!

Other refuge have I none;
    Hangs my helpless soul on thee;
Leave, ah! leave me not alone,
    Still support and comfort me!
All my trust on thee is stay'd,
    All my help from thee I bring:
Cover my defenceless head
    With the shadow of thy wing!

Wilt thou not regard my call?
    Wilt thou not accept my prayer?
Lo! I sink, I faint, I fall –
    Lo! on thee I cast my care!
Reach me out thy gracious hand:
    While I of thy strength receive,
Hoping against hope, I stand,
    Dying, and behold I live!

Plenteous grace with thee is found,
    Grace to cover all my sin;
Let the healing streams abound;
    Make and keep me pure within:
Thou of life the Fountain art,
    Freely let me take of thee;
Spring thou up within my heart,
    Rise to all eternity!

Charles Wesley (1707-88)

PART IV
THE REDEMPTION AND THE JOY

4:1–12
7. Love beyond law

Boaz' masterstroke (4:1–6)

And Boaz went up to the gate and sat down there; and behold, the next of kin, of whom Boaz had spoken, came by. So Boaz said, 'Turn aside, friend; sit down here'; and he turned aside and sat down. ²And he took ten men of the elders of the city, and said, 'Sit down here'; so they sat down. ³Then he said to the next of kin, 'Naomi, who has come back from the country of Moab, is selling the parcel of land which belonged to our kinsman Elimelech. ⁴So I thought I would tell you of it, and say, Buy it in the presence of those sitting here, and in the presence of the elders of my people. If you will redeem it, redeem it; but if you will not, tell me, that I may know, for there is no one besides you to redeem it, and I come after you.' And he said, 'I will redeem it.' ⁵Then Boaz said, 'The day you buy the field from the hand of Naomi, you are also buying Ruth the Moabitess, the widow of the dead, in order to restore the name of the dead to his inheritance.' ⁶Then the next of kin said, 'I cannot redeem it for myself, lest I impair my own inheritance. Take my right of redemption yourself, for I cannot redeem it.'

The focus of attention now moves to the city *gate*, in many ways the very centre of city life. Here the townsfolk gather for conversation,[1] and for the administration of justice.[2] At the gate the poor wait for aid.[3] Here business is transacted. It was 'at the gate' that Abraham negotiated to buy the cave of Machpelah from Ephron.[4] 'At the gate' Hamor and Shechem traded with the sons of Jacob.[5] It is at the gate

---

[1] *Cf.* Ps. 127:5.
[2] Am. 5:10; Dt. 22:15, 24; *cf.* E. W. Heaton, *The Hebrew Kingdoms* (OUP, 1968), p. 203.
[3] Pr. 22:22.   [4] Gn. 23:10.   [5] Gn. 34:20.

that the elders of society meet,[6] the princes and the nobles, the young
and the old.[7] And today Boaz goes to the gate to take his seat with the
others. He is on the look-out for the 'next of kin' of whom he spoke to
Ruth. From what transpires, it is clear that he has a subtle plan of
action ready in his mind.

When the next of kin appeared, Boaz called to him in a friendly
tone, and urged him to join him. Then he called together a group of
ten elders to act as witnessing judges of the transaction he was about to
propose.[8] The elders would customarily validate contracts and trade
agreements by responding to this formal call to be a 'witness' – an
important function in the business life of the people,[9] which conferred
binding authority on the transactions. It was written in the law [10] that
the elders of a city are particularly charged with jurisdiction in matters
of family rights such as the levirate.

It is at this point in the narrative that the problems for the reader
begin to multiply! We are left with a number of questions to which we
can only guess at answers. Boaz introduces a new factor into the
pattern that our author has woven up until this point: one that is at
first rather surprising, but one which, as we shall see, turns out to be
what Rowley called Boaz' 'masterstroke'.[11] Boaz talks about land
purchase. '*Naomi, who has come back from the country of Moab*,' says Boaz
to the other near kinsman, '*is selling the parcel of land which belonged to our
kinsman Elimelech.*' This is the first we have heard of the *land*. Possibly
Boaz and Naomi have talked together after Ruth's night-time visit,
and this plan of action is the result. We are not told the details of the
relation between the sale of the land and the marriage of Ruth. We do
not know why Naomi came into this property in the first place. We are
only told that it *belonged to Elimelech*. Perhaps the field was a gift to
Naomi from Elimelech before he died. But if she owned it then, why
do we hear nothing of it before? Why did Ruth have to go out to glean?
Why was there no livelihood available from this land? De Vaux
suggests that Naomi was perhaps acting as guardian over the rights to
the land of Elimelech's late sons, Mahlon and Chilion, and certainly
Ruth 4:9 describes the land as being jointly owned by them. Perhaps
now, in the extremity of her poverty, Naomi is being forced to sell the
land – land which she could then seek to persuade a goel to redeem for
her.[12] Perhaps, as Gunkel suggests,[13] in her absence in Moab the land
had been confiscated. And maybe, rather like the widow in a similar

---

[6] Pr. 31:23.   [7] Jb. 29:7–10.   [8] *Cf.* Jos. 20:4.
[9] *Cf.* 1 Sa. 12:5; *cf.* also Is. 44:8.
[10] Dt. 25:7–9.   [11] Rowley, p. 190.
[12] Lv. 25:23f.   [13] Gunkel, quoted in Leggett, p. 221.

111

position referred to in 2 Kings 8:1–6, who appealed to the king for her property to be returned to her, Naomi now wants someone to act on her behalf for the return of the field. If Boaz would act as her representative, she could claim her land back, and then proceed to sell it for revenue.

Alternatively, perhaps the levirate was itself connected in some way with land inheritance. The book of Numbers suggests that widows were not included in the list of those who could inherit property from a man who died without leaving a male heir.[14] (Indeed it has been suggested, therefore, that the practice of allowing widows to inherit land developed late on in the history of Israel.[15]) But we could understand the law in Numbers by supposing that the deceased's property passed to his brothers via the levirate. In the case of Naomi, also, perhaps the levirate and land inheritance were connected. At the time of her husband's death, we recall, Naomi was in Moab. She seems to have come home to Bethlehem soon after her sons had died. Perhaps the question of land ownership had to await the settlement of the levirate transactions. And now at last the way seems open for a goel to enter into a levirate-type marriage with Ruth. Maybe Boaz has shared with Naomi his own love for Ruth, and the difficulty of the fact that there is a nearer kinsman on whom the goel responsibilities would fall. Together, we may imagine, Boaz and Naomi have sought a way round this dilemma, and by using the goel responsibilities for land redemption wish to make it very difficult for this nearer kinsman to enter a levirate marriage with Ruth. This – as we shall see – is what happened.

What is clear, amid all these uncertainties, is that Naomi had an undisputed right to sell this field, and that Boaz is choosing this moment, the day after Ruth's night-time request to him at the threshing floor, to raise the matter with this the nearest of Elimelech's kinsmen.

As Rowley comments helpfully on all this:

It is idle to speculate on the amount of property Naomi had. It has been suggested that it may have been barely sufficient to maintain Naomi, and therefore insufficient to maintain Naomi and Ruth. It may have been less or more than this. But it seems likely that the property was but a counter in the game, and that Boaz skilfully used it to secure his end. It is improbable that the property had been

---

[14] Nu. 27:8–11.

[15] Cooke refers to Judith 8:7 as evidence for this. The husband was allowed to insert a clause into the marriage settlement, giving his widow the right to dwell in his house after him and so be nourished from his wealth. *Cf.* Talmud *Kethuboth* 4. 8.

effectively occupied by Naomi since her return. For she arrived back at the beginning of the barley harvest, which had barely been gathered in by the time the story reaches its climax. It is unlikely that the usufruct of the property had been enjoyed by Elimelech and his heirs during the years of Naomi's sojourn in Moab, and probable that it had been farmed by other members of the family who had enjoyed its fruits. It may even have been that Naomi was unaware of her title to it, or that she would have been powerless to secure possession but for the support of Boaz. But Boaz knew of her legal right to it, and used it for his purpose. How she came to have this legal right escapes us, since we are not told elsewhere of the inheritance rights of widows without living children. But that she had a title to an unspecified amount of property is quite clear.'[16]

So the first refusal of the opportunity to redeem Naomi's land, now that for whatever reason she chose to sell, belongs to the nearest of kin, and Boaz now offers it to him in the presence of the elders at the gate (4:4). If he will not act as goel to redeem the land, Boaz says that he will redeem it instead.

We are not clear whether this nearest kinsman realized that a double duty fell on him as goel, both to buy the land and to assume levirate responsibilities for the widow. We may assume, though, that he realized that had Naomi been a younger woman, he would have been expected to enter a levirate marriage with her, but that now she was past child-bearing age there was no chance of a levirate child·being born, to whom the property would revert. He therefore thinks that the land would be his, and for his heirs, and so agrees to redeem it.

At this point in the narrative, Boaz declares his hand: no, it is not Naomi whom you would have to consider with regard to the levirate, but her daughter-in-law, Ruth. 'The day you buy the field from the hand of Naomi, you are also acquiring Ruth the Moabitess';[17] and that for the specific purpose of raising a son in order to restore the name of the dead to his inheritance. It was obviously accepted that Ruth, of marriageable and child-bearing age, would replace Naomi in the levirate responsibility of raising a child to Elimelech.

The kinsman was now placed in a predicament – which was exactly what Boaz had intended! Here Boaz' deep personal care for Ruth shines through. It was in order that he might marry her that Boaz had engineered this ploy, mentioning the land first, and Ruth afterwards. And his 'masterstroke' came off. He skilfully used the possibilities of

[16] Rowley, pp. 183f.

[17] The RSV renders the word 'buying', but 'acquiring' would make better sense.

the law to place the nearest kinsman in an impossible position. The unnamed goel now realized that he had two responsibilites and not one, and that both belonged together. He had a responsibility to Elimelech's property, and a responsibility to the widow of one of Elimelech's sons. Since he was the nearest of kin on whom both responsibilities fell, he could hardly accept one without the other. 'Either he must play the part of the kinsman, or he must not.'[18]

Usually, we may suppose, if a man left property and a widow, the kinsman would marry the widow but not need to buy the property. He might have to provide some support for the widow, but in due course the land would become the property of the levirate son, the legal heir of the dead man. In this case, however, the question of land purchase has been linked with that of levirate duty – as is properly lawful if unexpected – but this, particularly with Ruth's lack of any means of support, would involve the kinsman in large financial outlay. Furthermore, the primary reason why this kinsman could not contemplate both goel responsibilities together was that to do so would *impair* his *own inheritance*. Had he just been required to redeem the land, he would be been financially poorer, but at least the land would be his. The only way he could lose it would be if (as he originally thought) a levirate son was born to Naomi, to whom the property would revert as legal heir of Elimelech. And that, as we have said, he realized was most unlikely. But if he were to marry *Ruth* and give her a levirate son, the property would revert to the son, and the kinsman would lose both his money and eventually the land. His own estate would be considerably weakened, and his own inheritance diminished. It was important for him, too, that his family name should not die with him. So he is forced to refuse the responsibilities of being goel, and hands the right of redemption over to Boaz.

All this illustrates, therefore, that to act as goel in these circumstances would be very costly. It involved personal sacrifice. The goel would have to give part of his own inheritance (the cost of the land) for the sake of others (Elimelech's family name and the inheritance of Elimelech's property). This would have to require an act of love and sacrifice which this kinsman was not in a position of offer.

We find, therefore, in the book of Ruth that the levirate practice seems to have been extended from the law which we find in Deuteronomy 25 and in the way it was effected in the story of Judah and Tamar in Genesis 38. It is also made clear that one of the responsibilities falling on the goel was that of marrying a childless widow in a

[18] Rowley, p. 185.

114

levirate marriage. As Leggett argues convincingly, these duties were obviously not understood in a legalistic way. There are legal duties prescribed in the Pentateuch, as we have seen, but 'the story of Ruth is the story of *hesed* motivating beyond the letter of the law. The laws were pointers or guides showing in concrete fashion how *hesed* might operate within the family.'[19] *Hesed* captures the spirit of the levirate law, and deepens and extends the law's provisions for the sake of the family welfare which the law was devised to protect. A. S. Herbert makes the same point in these words: 'Perhaps... it is deliberately intended that the action of Boaz "goes beyond" the tradition suggested by the Judah and Tamar story and what is required by the law of Deuteronomy 25:5–10.' It is by such fulfillings of the law, Herbert suggests, that the religion of the people of God is saved from becoming legalistic.[20]

Motivated by his own love for Ruth and his willingness — and ability — to give his money for Ruth's sake and that of the name of Elimelech, Boaz has cleverly placed the nearer kinsman in a situation in which he can do nothing other than offer right of redemption to him, Boaz, the next in line (4:6). There was nothing illegal here, nor underhand. It simply underlines in a marked way the voluntary nature of the responsibilities of the goel in this narrative, and the way his act called for the highest degree of commitment, love and personal sacrifice. The significance of Boaz' 'wealth', to which we referred in Ruth 2:1, now becomes plain. The kinsman-redeemer has to be related to those in need, has to be able to help. He has also to be willing to sacrifice in order to do so. He is under no obligation. His act is an act of love.

Witness a marriage (4:7–10)

Now this was the custom in former times in Israel concerning redeeming and exchanging: to confirm a transaction, the one drew off his sandal and gave it to the other, and this was the manner of attesting in Israel. [8]*So when the next of kin said to Boaz, 'Buy it for yourself,' he drew off his sandal.* [9]*Then Boaz said to the elders and all the people, 'You are witnesses this day that I have bought from the hand of Naomi all that belonged to Elimelech and all that belonged to Chilion and to Mahlon.* [10]*Also Ruth the Moabitess, the widow of Mahlon, I have bought to be my wife, to perpetuate the name of the dead in his inheritance, that the name of the dead may not be cut off from among his brethren and from the gate of his native place; you are witnesses this day.'*

[19] Leggett, pp. 248f.   [20] *Peake's Commentary on the Bible*, 'Ruth', p. 316.

115

One point of particular importance now comes to light in this paragraph: *Boaz marries Ruth*. Not until now has anything further than the levirate duty been spoken of. This levirate duty did not always imply full marriage. In the case of Judah and Tamar, there was no marriage. We do not know whether the near kinsman who has just expressed his inability to act as goel would have entered a full marriage with Ruth, or only acted as her levir until a child was born. He may already have been married himself, with an inheritance to safeguard for the sake of his own children. But with Boaz the situation is different. Rowley thinks it highly likely that Boaz was childless. Probably he was a bachelor. He may have been a widower. He was certainly an older man, a man of wealth and influence. He had said that he was honoured that Ruth should have approached him rather than sought out the younger men of the town. And now he seeks not only to fulfil his responsibilities as levir: he takes Ruth to be his wife.

We can imagine the scene: with not just *the elders* only, but *all the people* called in to witness what is going on. There is a note of celebration in the air, to judge from the people's response (4:11–12). The ceremony of the shoe [21] was enacted (a custom apparently fallen into disuse by the time our author was writing). By this means a transaction (in this case the transfer of rights from the kinsman to Boaz) was validated: one of the parties removed his *sandal* and gave it to the other. By this means the kinsman abandoned his right of redemption in favour of Boaz.

In the Deuteronomic law concerning the duties of the levir,[22] when the levir refused to do his duty, his sandal was removed from him – he was stripped of his rights, as a mark of public humiliation. In Ruth 4, however, the mood is rather one of joy. And *all the people* are involved in the celebration. This is an aspect to marriage which should not be lost. In our day, marriage is coming to be thought of by some only as a private alliance between two people, to be made (and even terminated) as they wish, by their private choice. But society has always had an interest in the formation of a new pair bond, and the growth of a new family unit in society. Despite the very different cultural surroundings,

[21] De Vaux (p. 169) suggests that the shoe serves as a probative instrument in the transfer of land. Ps. 60:8, 'Upon Edom I cast my shoe', seems to indicate 'taking possession'. He says, 'At Nuzu, the seller lifted his foot off the ground he was selling, and placed the buyer's foot on it. Here too, a pair of shoes (and a garment) appears as a fictitious payment to convalidate certain irregular transactions. This may explain, in Amos 2:6; 8:6, the poor man who is sold, or bought, for a pair of sandals: he has been unjustly dispossessed while the exaction has been given a cloak of legality. Here in Ruth 4, however, the transaction is fully legal and properly witnessed.'

[22] Dt. 25:5f.

expectancies of marriage, and social relationships between the sexes, the covenant model of marriage which we can discern in both Old and New Testaments carries with it the fact that 'marriage' is to be understood *both* in personal and relational terms, when we focus on the couple, *and* in social terms, when we stand back from the couple and see their place in the wider social group. One of the three bases on which the marriage covenant stands, as expounded in simplest terms by the narrator of Genesis 2:24 ('leaving father and mother', 'cleaving to wife', 'becoming one flesh'), makes this clear. The 'leaving' is a public declaration that a marriage is being made. It is the occasion on which the couple together receive the public support of their friends and society in the new social unit which they are creating. It is the occasion on which the couple also accept their vocation to be a new unit within society – to live out in society a relationship which in some way mirrors God's covenant relationship with his people. In one of Bonhoeffer's sermons he says this:

> Marriage is more than your love for each other. It has a higher dignity and power, for it is God's holy ordinance... In your love you see only the heaven of your happiness, but in marriage you are placed at a post of responsibility towards the world and mankind. Your love is your own private possession, but marriage is something more than personal – it is a status, an office... that joins you together in the sight of God and man.[23]

Today's questions, 'Why get married?', 'Why bother with the piece of paper?', are to be answered in terms of responsibility to society, and a recognition that our equivalent of *the elders and all the people* have a proper interest in the formation of a new family group.

Public witness is always an aspect of covenant-making. And the social importance of public witness retains this aspect of the meaning of marriage. But there is a personal value here also. The public witness serves among other things as a buttress in a marriage against disintegration in those times when the relationship is under strain. It is a constant reminder that promises were made, obligations entered into, and prayer for grace and resources asked. The vows were not simply a private matter, but publicly made and publicly witnessed. A sense of accountability to the wider Christian fellowship helps us to maintain our promises and acts to support us in the harder times when our commitment to loving faithfulness is put to the test.

[23] Quoted in L. Smedes, *Sex in the Real World* (Lion, 1976), p. 176.

The importance of celebration is not be minimized either! Lewis Smedes, in his excellent book *Sex in the Real World*, writes this:

> There is one more thing about marriage that asks for a wedding: it is the human need for festivity. Human life seems to need moments set apart for celebration and partying. We mark birthdays, anniversaries, graduations, births and any other special event in our lives by breaking the routine of our life-style with a party. A person needs something to make toasts to; so does the community. And weddings are festivals celebrating the beginning of a new adventure. God's blessing on a marriage, given at a wedding, is really an act of celebration: the wedding affirms that a good and important thing is taking place... Weddings are the public beginnings of a new enterprise, which is at its heart the original private enterprise. Like all private enterprises, it needs the support and restraint of a community. Weddings are not society's trick to keep young people in line with custom; they are this society's method of receiving a new enterprise of love into its midst. [24]

For Boaz at the city gate, the celebration began without Ruth even being there! But 'all the people' were present, not only to witness, but to offer their prayers.

Prayer for blessing (4:11–12)

Then all the people who were at the gate, and the elders, said, 'We are witnesses. May the Lord make the woman, who is coming into your house, like Rachel and Leah, who together built up the house of Israel. May you prosper in Ephrathah and be renowned in Bethlehem; [12]*and may your house be like the house of Perez, whom Tamar bore to Judah, because of the children that the Lord will give you by this young woman.'*

The immediate response of the people to this demonstration of redeeming love is twofold: to witness and to pray. To be a witness in this context, G. A. F. Knight reminds us, 'means to speak of it to others, and to allow it to be clearly seen in one's own behaviour and attitude to the rest of mankind.' [25] He points us to the similarities of thought between many of the aspects of the book of Ruth, and the thinking of the later chapters of the prophecy of Isaiah. 'I, I am the Lord, and besides me there is no saviour... and you are my witnesses, says the

---

[24] Smedes, *ibid.*, p. 146.   [25] Knight, p. 41.

Lord.'[26] And a little later on, the prophet reminds the people, 'It is too light a thing that you should be my servant to raise up the tribes of Jacob and to restore the preserved of Israel; I will give you as a light to the nations, that my salvation may reach to the end of the earth.'[27]

Through the self-sacrificing act of Boaz, Ruth had been established as belonging within the people of God. Boaz had expressed in practice himself what he believed to be true of God's action towards his people. That is always the calling of the people of God; people who are redeemed are to be the agents through whom others find redemption. To this the people bear their witness.

This witness is coupled with prayer for God's blessing on the new family. How much this small book throbs with the life of prayer! Naomi's response to the news from Bethlehem that the famine had ended was to send her daughter-in-law back to their Moabite homes with prayer (1:8). The routine greeting Boaz offered his workers, and their reply, was a prayer (2:4). Boaz' generous welcome to Ruth to glean in his field was made as a prayer (2:12). And Naomi prayed in thanksgiving in glad reaction to Ruth's return home with her news about Boaz at the end of the day's gleaning (2:20). Boaz responded to Ruth's night-time visit with a prayer (3:10). And now all the people respond with prayer to the transaction at the gate by seeking God's blessing on Boaz and on Ruth. How clearly all this illustrates the deep spirituality of the author of this book. Every aspect of life, from misery to joy, from the routine to the extraordinary, daily work and social intercourse, as well as the very private moments, are lived in the faith that God is there and God cares. Not only so, but human actions, as we have seen, themselves point to the character of God. We have noted the way in which Boaz' ḥeseḏ corresponds with the ḥeseḏ of Yahweh. It is interesting also to recall the way in which the human marriage covenant of man with wife is often used as an analogy of the relationship of God with his covenant people, and, 'by reciprocal illumination',[28] how God's covenant gives a pattern and a meaning to human married life. Indeed, all human relationships are to be patterned on, and in turn reveal, something of the way God makes relationships in his covenanted dealings with his people.

Here now, the people's prayer brings an awareness of the hand of God into the dealings at the gate. And as Knight points out, this has implications for the way the author of this book thought of God. The way he tells the whole action of Boaz as goel, redeeming the land and

[26] Is. 43:11–12.   [27] Is. 49:6.
[28] A phrase from E. Schillebeeckx, *Marriage: Human Reality and Saving Mystery* (Sheed & Ward, 1965), p. 33.

offering the family of Elimelech a future and a hope through his own commitment in marriage to Ruth – all this points to the author's understanding of the character of God. For if a mere man, a creature of God, could act like this, showing his power to redeem an outcast and bring her into fellowship with the living God, then surely, says Knight, the author must see God as at least as compassionate to all the Ruths (of Moab, of Babylon, and of every other land), and God himself must be a 'God of redemption with the desire and the power to redeem all outcasts into fellowship with himself.'[29]

It is to this God that the hearts of the people now turn in prayer. They have been witnesses of an act of redeeming love. They now seek God's blessing. And their concern for Boaz and for his new wife and family is threefold.

First, the wife: *May the Lord make the woman, who is coming into your house, like Rachel and Leah, who together built up the house of Israel.* Rachel and Leah were the two wives of Jacob, and from their children, and the children born to Jacob's concubines who in some way also became their children, the whole nation of Israel was descended. May Ruth, too, become the ancestress of a famous race. May she have many descendants within the family and purpose of God.

Then the husband: *May you prosper in Ephrathah and be renowned in Bethlehem.* May Boaz himself be enriched through this marriage, and his offspring. May he achieve might and be famous. As Cooke translates: 'let thy name be proclaimed'. Not only are we concerned with maintaining the name of Elimelech. Through this full marriage to Ruth, Boaz' own family name will be established also.

Finally the family-to-be: *May your house be like the house of Perez.* Perez is presumably mentioned for several reasons. The first is that he was the more important of the twin sons of the levirate relationship between Judah and Tamar. The parallel to this situation is clear. But more than that, Perez is therefore one of the ancestors of the Bethlehemites who descended from Judah.[30] The expression *house of Perez* points probably to the large number of his descendants – of whom the people at the gate are some. Perez was certainly one of Boaz' ancestors.[31] The people pray that Boaz will, like his ancestor, have a numerous and renowned family of descendants. And if, as has been suggested and seems more than likely, Boaz was childless, the 'children that the Lord will give you by this young woman' mentioned in the prayer, would be heirs not only to Elimelech, but to Boaz himself.

[29] Knight, p. 41.   [30] 1 Ch. 2:5, 18, 50f.
[31] Ru. 4:18. *Cf.* 1 Ch. 2:2–12ff.; Mt. 1:2–6.

4:13–22

8. We have a history

'One flesh' (4:13)

So Boaz took Ruth and she became his wife; and he went in to her, and the Lord gave her conception, and she bore a son.

The primary biblical picture of marriage is that of *covenant*. God's covenant relations with his people are described in marriage language; human married life derives its meaning from, and is to be patterned on, God's covenant relation with his people, Christ's with his church.[1] We can discern three main elements to the marriage covenant: the promise of committed love between husband and wife; the public covenant-making by which a new family unit is created in society; and the developing personal communion between the partners in relationship, which sexual union symbolizes and deepens. The writer of Genesis 2:24 expresses this in his comment on the narrative of the creation of woman as partner to the man: 'Therefore a man leaves his father and his mother and cleaves to his wife, and they become one flesh.' For Boaz, all three parts of the marriage covenant are now together: his love for Ruth, the public witness to their wedding, and now the sexual union.

In the thinking of our author and other biblical writers, physical sexual union belongs within such a context of a committed, loving, and publicly known relationship. This was not only to safeguard the rights of children. It was part of the meaning of 'one flesh' – that developing understanding which we can trace through both Old and New Testaments that marriage means 'a complete unitary partnership of one man with one woman for life, symbolised by and deepened through the sexual relationship.'[2] As Paul for his time also makes clear

[1] *Cf.* D. J. Atkinson, *To Have and To Hold* (Collins, 1979), ch. 3.
[2] *Ibid. Cf.* P. Ramsey, *One Flesh* (Grove, 1975).

121

in writing to the Corinthians,[3] sexual union involves much more than bodily union. It creates, sustains and symbolizes the 'one flesh' committed partnership of man and wife to each other. Body-life is one with emotional and spiritual life. To separate them is – at some point – to live a sexual lie.

In our day, in which, through effective contraception, the relational and procreative aspects of our sexuality can be separated in practice, it is often assumed that the physical aspect of sexual relationship can be separated from all other aspects. But that is not the biblical view. The Bible rather urges on us the question: Does sexual union mean 'I give myself to you', as the physical relationship clearly says it does? Then, if there is no corresponding emotional and spiritual self-giving in a sexual relationship, are we seeking to divide what God has joined together? Further, as Jack Dominian argues so well, the 'sustaining, healing and growth' which are some of the blessings available in a good marriage relationship under God, require a framework of 'continuity, reliability and predictability' – that is permanence – in which to develop.[4] The permanence of the covenant between God and his people is again our model here. The richness of the God-given significance to physical sexual relationship requires a context of permanent and committed love and faithfulness between the partners. That is why biblical morality – while affirming our sexuality at all levels of personal encounter – reserves the full physical expression of love in sexual intercourse for the one context of a permanent heterosexual commitment of faithful love.

That is the picture that has been built up for us of the marriage of Boaz and Ruth.

The gift of life

From the prayer which the elders have just offered, it is clear that they regarded children as a gift from God. This is underlined by our author's comment here. He does not simply relate the human events: *He went in to her* (the usual Old Testament expression for sexual intercourse)... *and she bore a son.* He joins the two events with this: *the Lord gave her conception.*

If there is one theme more than any other which dominates the book of Ruth, it is that of the over-ruling providence of God, and our human dependence on him. God is the source of life. Life, and its

---

[3] 1 Cor. 6:12ff.
[4] J. Dominian, *Marriage, Faith and Love* (Darton, Longman and Todd, 1981), p. 89.

blessings, are a gift from his hand. And particularly here, the conception of a child is understood as a gift of God.

At what point does personal human life begin? The biblical witness replies unequivocally: at conception. And many modern secular thinkers agree. At conception all the human genes are present, and though some time must elapse before the development of the cerebral cortex upon the functioning of which truly human capacity for personal response depends, nonetheless in the newly conceived foetus, we are in the presence of, at the very least, a human person in process of becoming. Increasing evidence is available that the early foetal experiences are very significant. Particularly in the first three months of foetal life, the health and well-being of the mother, and the experiences of the foetus through her, have a marked effect on the developing personality.[5]

This is a far cry from the 'products of conception' and 'womb tissue' language which has become the jargon of some of the pro-abortion propaganda. Even if there were any doubt concerning the status of the nascent life in the womb, the burden of proof would lie heavily on anyone who decided that the foetus should not be given the benefit of the doubt.

But the biblical witness leaves no doubt. There are many biblical allusions to human life before birth.[6] Even the agnosticism of the Preacher ('You do not know how a pregnant woman comes to have a body and a living spirit in her womb; nor do you know how God, the maker of all things, works'), contains an affirmation: the womb contains not only a 'body' but a 'living spirit'.[7] The pentateuchal law framed to protect the pregnant woman and foetal life requires that if a woman is forced to go into premature labour because of a brawl in which she has inadvertently been knocked, compensation is due to her in the form of a fine; if either she or the child is harmed 'then you shall give life for life'.[8] The killing of the unborn was regarded in ancient Israel as 'barbarous cruelty, calling down God's judgment'.[9] Jeremiah bears witness to the call of God: 'Before I formed you in the womb I knew you for my own',[10] as does Paul in his recognition that God had called him from his birth.[11] In Psalm 139, the psalmist recalls that he

[5] Cf. e.g. F. Lake, *Tight Corners in Pastoral Counselling* (Darton, Longman and Todd, 1981).

[6] Cf. the pamphlet 'Biblical Allusions to Life Before Birth', by Harley Smyth (Christian Medical Fellowship).

[7] Ec. 11:5 NEB.   [8] Ex. 21:22f.

[9] Cf. A. Cole, *Exodus* (Tyndale Old Testament Commentaries, Inter-Varsity Press, 1973), p. 169, referring to 2 Ki. 15:16.

[10] Je. 1:5 NEB.   [11] Gal. 1:15; cf. also Ps. 51:5.

is fully known by God from his time in the womb. Furthermore, the opening chapter of Luke's Gospel seems to show that there is an indication in the life of John the Baptist of some prenatal determination of personality and character. 'By the ordinance and gift of God, a new life is conceived – a fresh creation, a life quite unique and irreplaceable, with a specific, identifiable personal destiny.'[12]

This is the faith expressed also by the author of Ruth. Conception is a gift from the Lord. Seen in this light, the whole abortion debate, argued as it often is in terms either of conflicting rights or of beneficial consequences, takes on a deeper dimension. If we are in the presence of a human person in process of becoming – a human being with a personal destiny under God from the moment of conception – the burden of proof lies heavily on those who decide to terminate a pregnancy. The question of abortion can be raised only within the category of the justifiable taking of a human life.

From emptiness to joy (4:14–17)

Then the women said to Naomi, 'Blessed be the Lord, who has not left you this day without next of kin; and may his name be renowned in Israel! [15]He shall be to you a restorer of life and a nourisher of your old age; for your daughter-in-law who loves you, who is more to you than seven sons, has borne him.' [16]Then Naomi took the child and laid him in her bosom, and became his nurse. [17]And the women of the neighbourhood gave him a name, saying, 'A son has been born to Naomi.' They named him Obed; he was the father of Jesse, the father of David.

The joyful outcome of the story: the son born to Ruth who is also therefore born to Naomi in the family of Elimelech, is again surrounded with prayers of thankfulness to God. It is this prayer which brings the story full circle, and proclaims again the providential rule and care of God. The focus is now back on Naomi. She left Moab bereft of her husband and her sons. She was greeted in Bethlehem by the women who saw her grief and heard her bitterness. They now share her joy: *Blessed be the Lord, who has not left you this day without next of kin!*

Again the sense of family solidarity is emphasized. The child was born to Ruth, *your daughter-in-law who loves you,* but he will also be to Naomi *a restorer of life and a nourisher of your old age.* As the levirate son for Mahlon, he is heir of Elimelech. Through him Elimelech's family name has not died out from that day to this. Through him God's

---

[12] Smyth, 'Biblical Allusions'.

purposes were carried forward. Ruth and Naomi were given a future and a hope. But the purposes of God on the wider canvas of world history have also been accomplished, as we shall see. Perhaps it was very appropriate that the child should have been named *Obed*: 'Servant' – the servant of the Lord.

The sense of history (4:18–22)

Now these are the descendants of Perez: Perez was the father of Hezron, [19]Hezron of Ram, Ram of Amminadab, [20]Amminadab of Nahshon, Nahshon of Salmon, [21]Salmon of Boaz, Boaz of Obed, [22]Obed of Jesse, and Jesse of David.

The Bible seems to have a lot of genealogies, and genealogies are often boring. They serve, however, to remind us of one very important fact which the Bible insists that we should not forget: our inter-connectedness as human beings with generations past. Each conception is a gift from God. But it is a gift within a context. At the level of our genetic inheritance and physical descent, we are in many respects the products of our history. We are who we are to some significant degree because of who our parents and grandparents were. Our history matters.

It is precisely this sense of history which is captured by an otherwise boring, and apparently tacked on, list of names at the end of this chapter. 'These are the descendants of' is the formula found elsewhere, in Genesis 2:4; 5:1, *etc.* It indicates the sense of a developing story. As Leon Morris comments; 'There is an air of history about this term.'[13]

So from Perez, one of the twin sons of Judah and Tamar, through various generations (some of which have probably been skipped over by the author), we come to Boaz, and so to Obed. Obed was the father of Jesse, who was himself the father of Israel's greatest king.

As Keil and Delitzsch comment, in one sense the genealogy 'forms not only the end, but the starting point, of the history contained in the book'. 'For even if we should not attach so much importance as to say with Auberlen that "the book of Ruth contains, as it were, the inner side, the spiritually moral background of the genealogies which play so significant a part even in the Israelitish antiquity", so much is un-questionably true, that the book contains a historical picture from the family life of the ancestors of David, intended to show how the ancestors of this great king walked uprightly before God and man in piety and singleness of heart, and in modesty and purity of life.' We can discern

[13] Morris, p. 316.

what they called the 'Messianic trait' also: 'that Ruth, a heathen woman, of a nation so hostile to the Israelites as that of Moab was, should have been thought worthy to be made the tribe-mother of the great and pious King David, on account of her faithful love to the people of Israel and her entire confidence in Jehovah, the God of Israel.'[14]

The historical continuity of the covenant purposes of God in the covenant people of God, from great father Abraham to the saving events of the life and death and resurrection of Jesus Christ, and beyond into the life and interconnectedness of the family of the Christian church – all this is brought to mind for us in the brief reference to the genealogy of Ruth in chapter 4, which centres on the child born to Boaz, by Ruth the daughter-in-law of Elimelech and Naomi.

We do well to remember the New Testament understanding of the Christian church as the historical covenant community, and the historical process as 'the sphere of God's sovereign providential rule'.[15] This should serve to deliver us from an overconcentration on individualistic faith, and remind us of our covenant links with believers in the past. It will help us to understand our Bibles as produced within the context of the covenant community; it will help us also to understand the traditions of the church – the historical communion of saints – as sharing in that same historical covenant context in its attempts to understand and apply biblical truth. The covenant family of God spans the centuries. It is to that family we are invited to belong.

We have rejected the suggestion that the whole purpose of the book of Ruth was to provide an ancestry for King David. But the author's decision to conclude his story in this way (and these verses are not obviously an addition to the text) underlines the fact that history for him was important. The whole life of the nation was bound up with their king. And the importance of kingship in Israel was tied to the life of the archetypal king, David. And his life, in terms of physical descent, was linked to the story of a Moabite girl gleaning in a barley field many miles from home; to a caring mother-in-law and a loving kinsman; to a night-time conversation at the threshing floor; to the willingness of a wealthy farmer to go beyond the requirements of law in his care for the needy. In short, it is in the ordinariness of the events of lives of ordinary people that God is working his purpose out. Future significant lives were bound up with the history of Ruth. And not only David's, but as Matthew takes care to remind us, that of our Lord Jesus himself.[16]

[14] Keil and Delitzsch, p. 466.

[15] *Cf.* N. T. Wright, *The Evangelical Anglican Identity Problem* (Latimer House, 1980), p. 26.

[16] Mt. 1:1, 5.

And when Christ our Saviour was born of David's line, in that same Bethlehem, he was born into a family of ordinary people. And they, too, by their willing obedience to the God who is gracious – focused most clearly in Mary's prayer, 'Behold, I am the handmaid of the Lord; let it be to me according to your word'[17] – were instruments of God's providential purposes in his world.

Our faith, our ordinary lives, our decisions too, are part of God's providential and gracious care. We today are part of the covenant family whose first father was Abraham, and which gave a welcome also to Ruth, the girl from Moab. We share in an interconnectedness of family life from their times until now. The God who called Ruth is the God who calls us in Christ. May we – like Ruth, and like Mary her great descendant – pledge our willing and loving obedience in response to God's gracious invitation to enjoy our place under the refuge of his wings.

[17] Lk. 1:38.

'The Lord be with you'

Our Father in heaven, Creator and Sustainer of your world, you hold all that you have made within your gracious providence. We thank you for the rich freedom you have given us. Help us in all things to see your hand, and to live as those whose lives are entrusted to your sovereign care. As Ruth from Moab became one of your people, so you call us by name and invite us home. We are glad to find shelter under the refuge of your wings.

In Jesus Christ, our Kinsman-Redeemer, you meet us in our ordinariness and make our human life your own. We thank you for your costly self-giving in redeeming love, setting us free to share the life of your family. You have taken our pains, our sin, our bitterness, our fear to yourself. Forgive us our sins, and teach us how to forgive. Grant that when, like Naomi, we walk the valley of tears in the evening and the dark, we may not lose sight of the resurrection dawn of hope and joy.

Through the Holy Spirit, the giver of life, you lead us into truth. You enrich the guidance of your law through the personal warmth of your generous love. As Boaz went beyond the call of duty in gracious provision for another's need, how much is your gift of grace far more abundant than we could ask or think! Teach us to be alert to the needs of others, and to work for a just distribution of the rich bounty of your world, that each may have daily bread for daily need.

God the Holy Trinity, from you each earthly family receives its name and learns its love. You are the God of history whose purposes span the centuries. Through your family the church you now make known your plan to unite all things in heaven and earth in Jesus Christ our Lord. Before him, one day, every knee will bow. We give you our praise, we ask for your aid, and we seek to bring all aspects of our lives under the rule of Christ our Lord. For from him and through him and to him are all things. To him be glory for ever.

Amen.